LIVE YOUR BEST LIFE

sponsored by:

Friends of the Jeff Davis County Library

Your
✓ physical
✓ emotional
✓ mental
✓ sexual
✓ social
health
A YOUNG ADULT
COLLECTION

The
V-Word

The
V-Word

True Stories about First-Time Sex

Amber J. Keyser

Simon Pulse

New York   London   Toronto   Sydney   New Delhi

 BEYOND WORDS

Hillsboro, Oregon

SIMON PULSE

An imprint of Simon & Schuster
Children's Publishing Division
1230 Avenue of the Americas
New York, NY 10020

BEYOND WORDS

20827 N.W. Cornell Road, Suite 500
Hillsboro, Oregon 97124-9808
503-531-8700 / 503-531-8773 fax
www.beyondword.com

This Beyond Words/Simon Pulse edition February 2016
Compilation and text copyright © 2016 by Amber J. Keyser
Cover copyright © 2016 by Beyond Words/Simon & Schuster, Inc.

Managing Editor: Lindsay S. Easterbrooks-Brown
Editor: Michelle McCann
Copyeditor: Jenefer Angell
Interior and cover design: Sara E. Blum
The text of this book was set in Bembo and Interstate.

SIMON PULSE is a trademark of Simon & Schuster, Inc., and the related logo is a registered
trademark of Simon & Schuster, Inc.
Beyond Words is an imprint of Simon & Schuster, Inc., and the Beyond Words logo is a
registered trademark of Beyond Words Publishing, Inc.

For information about special discounts for bulk purchases, please contact Simon & Schuster
Special Sales at 1-866-506-1949 or business@simonandschuster.com.

The Simon & Schuster Speakers Bureau can bring authors to your live event.
For more information or to book an event contact the Simon & Schuster Speakers Bureau
at 1-866-248-3049 or visit our website at www.simonspeakers.com.

Manufactured in the United States of America

10 9 8 7 6 5 4 3 2

Library of Congress Cataloging-in-Publication Data

The V-word : true stories about first-time sex / [edited by] Amber J. Keyser.
    pages   cm
Includes bibliographical references and index.
1. First sexual experiences. 2. Virginity. 3. Sex. I. Keyser, Amber.
HQ21.V185 2016
306.7—dc23

2015019131

ISBN 978-1-58270-590-3 (hc)
ISBN 978-1-58270-521-7 (pbk)
ISBN 978-1-4814-2729-6 (eBook)

Copyright page continued on pages 190–197.

{ For all the young women crossing the threshold: }
You are brave. You are worthy. You are good.

Contents

Preface

Virginity—it's a loaded word.

We women are told that virginity is something that makes us pure. Virginity is a thing to protect. A thing another person will eventually take away. It goes hand in hand with a host of other, crueler words. If we give it away, we're called sluts. If we hang on to it, we're called prudes. Once it's lost, something is gone forever. Some *thing*?

Virginity isn't a possession locked behind a chastity belt or spread wide on silken sheets. It's not a ripe cherry waiting to be plucked, popped, or eaten. Virginity is a state of being. Being a virgin means standing on one side of an experience, not yet having walked through the door. Crossing the threshold is far more about gaining something than about losing it.

It feels like a big deal and in many ways it is. Sexual experiences put us in the closest possible contact with another person. Tongues circle. Thighs press and squeeze. Hands caress breasts. Bodies slide together. As our bodies merge, the boundaries between us melt away. We are vulnerable.

Intense emotions swirl through the sexual experience. Are we powerful or powerless? Loved or used? Good or bad? The selves we bring into sex—our values, our upbringing, our history—will shape the experience. If we're not attentive, the ramifications of having sex could change the course of our lives—pregnancy, sexually transmitted infections, emotional trauma. We could also be filled with desire, thrilled by pleasure, deeply connected to another person, and empowered by the beautiful strength of our own bodies.

Navigating this complexity isn't easy, especially in a world where we are bombarded with mixed messages about sex: *Do as I say. Be quiet. Do what I did. Stay pure. Be sexy. Make others happy. Do the right thing.* I wrote this book to start a different kind of conversation. I asked smart, honest women to share their stories about first sexual experiences.

The V-Word is not a how-to manual, urging you to run out and have sex. Nor is it supposed to scare you into abstinence. Rather, we hope that it will convince you to think broadly about the many ways women can express and respect the sexual side of themselves.

If you decide to become sexually active, I urge you to get informed by visiting websites like Scarleteen.com and reading books like *S-E-X: The All-You-Need-To-Know Progressive Sexuality Guide to Get You through High School and College* by Heather Corinna. At the end of this book you'll find many resources, including more books and websites.

And if you decide to wait, that's okay too.

All the experiences in *The V-Word* really happened. Names and identifying details have been changed but besides that every story within these pages is true or at least as true as memory can make them. We write about straight sex and queer sex. We write about diving in and about waiting. Some of our first times were exhilarating, others disappointing, some surprising. Some happened too soon, others at exactly the right moment. But no matter the specifics of the situation, our first times stayed with us.

We don't intend to tell you what to do. Instead, we share our own truths and leave your choices in your own capable hands. We don't think sex is dirty or shameful or immoral, but it's not insignificant either. Every first time, and there are many, is something to linger over. There's no need to rush. Good sex is ripe with giving and receiving, with mutual desire and respect. It can be a force for good in the universe and in our own lives.

The opposite of virgin turns out to be a vast world of possible experiences, a lifetime of getting to know our sexual selves and sharing them with others.

It's not all or nothing.

It's not a direct line.

It's a journey.

And along the way women have discovered that there is a V-word far more powerful than virginity—VOICE.

Whether you say *yes* or *no* to sexual experiences, finding your voice—and using it—is the most important part of becoming the person you want to be.

Girls get hot.

That's the truth.

It's not just the guys with their constant boners. It's us too. We get turned on. We fantasize. We touch ourselves. Sometimes we touch each other. All this wild girl horniness is perfectly normal. Humans are lots of things—thinkers, nurturers, fighters—but we are also sexual beings.

Our bodies are magnificent. I don't mean what they look like. I'm talking about what they do and how they feel. Fingers seek the soft-hard-rough-smooth skin of the body. Limbs entwine with arms-legs-hands. Our bodies provide us with so much pleasure, sensations that many of us come to know at a very early age, as I describe in the first story.

1
Wanting Everything
Amber J. Keyser

I had a kid's body—no hips, hardly any breasts, hardly more than pubic hair peach fuzz. I'd never had a period or a boyfriend or a date for a middle school dance. It was the summer after eighth grade and I was abuzz with physical desire. I'd known for a long time that it felt good to touch myself, and years earlier I'd played kissing games with neighborhood girls, but now, as I careened toward puberty, my body was a constant source of *wow*.

When it came to sex, I had zero experience but a lot of book learning. We had moved the summer before seventh grade. Among my mother's discarded books on a garage sale table, I found my textbook—an explicit memoir by a sex-loving prostitute. Heart racing, I'd pinched it off the table and snuck it to my room, reading and rereading her bawdy accounts of sex with both men and women. Her uninhibited attitude painted sex as a healthy and positive part of adult life. If it felt good and everyone wanted to do it then anything was a go.

By accident, I discovered just the right way to ride my bike so that the seat vibrated against the mound of my crotch. It seemed my panties were always damp, and I masturbated often—in the bath, in the hot tub, in my bed at night. I imagined what it would feel like to have oral sex. But in this stew of horniness, I also worried that something was wrong with me for thinking about sex so much. I watched the girls at school that everyone said were *doing it*. Were their bodies constantly on fire like mine? Or was I freak?

But arousal was constantly sneaking up on me. I crushed on actors in movies, characters in books, and Jason, a gawky boy who lived down the street. At school, Jason and I ignored each other—he, no doubt, because of my bottom-rung social status, and I because that's what you do to avoid humiliation in the halls of middle school. After school, we were less frosty. With a handful of other kids, we rode bikes through the golf course at the center of our neighborhood, infuriating men in plaid pants, and played tennis on the old, cracked courts. Jason and I snuck away to kiss in the tunnel at the neighborhood playground.

I wasn't thinking about having actual sex with him but the kissing sent heat coursing through me. I wondered what it would feel like to have him touch me. When my younger cousin crashed her bike and Jason carried her home like some knight in shorts and sneakers, I wished it were me bleeding at the knees and leaning against his chest. I took every opportunity to hang out with him, waiting to be alone, wanting more kissing.

Toward the end of the summer, I was house-sitting for an old lady who lived in a condo nearby. One day I dragged Jason and two of our friends along with me to check on the dog, and there they were—empty bedrooms, open beds, and not a single chance of discovery. A surprise, believe it or not.

I hadn't planned any of this.

There was no forethought, no real thinking at all.

My brain had vacated the building but my body was full speed ahead.

We paired off, our friends upstairs and me and Jason in a guest room with white carpet, a red bedspread, and tacky furniture detailed in gold paint. His lips were as soft as I remembered from the playground, his face pre-shaving smooth. We had our clothes off in moments. How did that even happen? My memory is a blur of color and texture. We slid into the cool sheets like otters sliding into the water.

What I remember is wanting everything.

His touch sent sizzling waves coursing over my body. This was nothing like when I masturbated. This was the best thing I had ever felt. My skin was electrified where we touched. Thigh to thigh, chest to chest. His arms around me. My hands in his hair. He smelled like boy and awesome.

I slid down under the covers, my cheek against his taut belly. And there was his penis. Hard inside but shockingly soft and smooth on the surface. I put my lips on the velvety end of his penis and took him in my mouth. After a while—who knows how much time passed—we changed places. And his mouth was hot and wet on the slit of my vulva. The new best thing ever.

When we were face to face again, we did not talk. We did not think. We did not consider protection or consequences. We were far too absorbed in good-yes-slick-hot-more-now to ask ourselves if we were ready. Instead we went to work figuring out how our parts fit together.

The problem was the parts.

Like mismatched puzzle pieces, they just wouldn't go together no matter how we twisted and writhed. His aim was terrible, and though I was aroused, my prepubescent body was also tight and unaccommodating. In the midst of this conundrum, our friends knocked on the door, ready to go. We scrambled, slightly dazed, out of the bed and back into our clothes. Jason and I hardly spoke, pretending, instead, that nothing had happened.

A few days later, his best friend asked me if we'd had sex. I didn't know what to say. Had we? There was no penetration. Nobody

came. I shrugged, noncommittal. He smirked, and I felt dirty. My
brain kicked back in and with it came shame and worry.

What kind of girl did that kind of thing? Was I a bad person?
How could I have gone so far without even thinking about pregnancy or disease? What if Jason had been less tender and had pushed
me beyond what I could do?

These were the thoughts that could have, and perhaps should
have, accompanied the yearnings of my body.

My brain finally caught up with the rest of me.

Jason and I never did anything like that again. In fact, I didn't
do anything sexual with anyone else for a long time, and I was
seventeen before I went all the way through with penetration. But
I often remember Jason and the lovely, rich pleasure we shared in
each other's bodies. We were young, that's true, but was it really
so wrong for us to kiss and touch and explore in a way that made
both of us feel so good?

I don't think so.

Did it count?

I wasn't sure if my explorations with Jason counted as sex. I'd always thought that losing my virginity had to involve penetration. But what about two women? If they're intimate with mouths-hands-vulvas and it feels great, is that sex? What about the straight couples who decide that they don't want to go all the way but everything else—all the other ways we can be sexual with each other—is considered okay? Are they still virgins?

It's common to talk about sex like it's binary. You've had it or you haven't. But what if sex is a spectrum of behaviors? In that context, the idea of virginity doesn't make a lot of sense. We humans don't have a sex switch that gets flipped from off to on, where it stays for the rest of our lives. Being sexually active means just that—you're participating in sexual activities with someone else. Maybe that happens for a while—weeks, months, years—and then maybe you step back from sex and move into abstinence for a time.

All along the way you get to make choices about what you want to do and when you want to stop. Sex isn't all or nothing, and, as you will see from Carrie's story, first times can sometimes surprise you.

{ Feeling through his body how good it feels. Tasting everything, smelling everything. }

{ Sweet, salty, sour, bitter. The way his body tenses. The way he breathes, soft, then hard. It's perfect. }

{ My body folds beneath him, shadowed. }

2
What Counts
Carrie Mesrobian

When it happened the first time, we were looking directly into each other's eyes. His blue eyes above me, me looking up at him, my childhood bed, the middle of the day, the shade open to a blue sunny sky. It was late spring and we'd been together since fall.

When he pushed his dick into me, it didn't hurt. We had a condom. I wasn't surprised. He was slow. I was ready. We had agreed to do this.

It was a lot like I'd expected it to feel. The same kind of pressure with his hands and fingers, really, only this time his hands were on either of my shoulders.

But something was wrong. It felt merely okay, not as intense as his fingers had felt up there. Nothing within me ached in happiness, like I'd been led to believe. I didn't feel changed. I knew we were both crossing over, from being virgins to being . . . not virgins. Whatever you call it when you're on the other side.

It felt like the way you might say the word "oh" when someone says something you don't care about.

Like, *Oh. Hmm. Well.*

Like, *Huh—that's what that space is for.*

Like, *Never used those muscles in my thighs in quite that way before. Interesting.*

Like, *Maybe it gets better, the longer it goes on?*

Finally, he interrupted these thoughts.

"Can you move your hips, maybe?"

He sounded embarrassed for me, so I moved my hips.

Then he moved with me and it was a little . . . different. But not by much. And, unlike everyone always said about it being over quick? It wasn't. It just kept going. Moving. The same bland way.

I suspected this was because I wasn't doing it right. Or I wasn't sexy enough. Or I'd done something else wrong.

Yet, I didn't lie or pretend that it felt good. I couldn't fake a feeling I didn't have, because by this time I knew I loved him: that was real. We'd said the words to each other, many times.

Except, this sex was *also* real. Something we'd put off and waited for and worried about. And after all that, it still wasn't good. I'd told him the truth about so many things but I'd never thought to tell him that, in my mind, having sex with a guy meant his penis would push some magic button inside me. That it would all feel so good and overwhelming that I'd lose control. There'd be no wandering thoughts. No questions.

Instead, I was staring up at him, my face blank and still, wondering when the miracle would occur.

He finally pulled out and chucked the condom. Nobody came. It seemed clear to me that this was a bad, horrible thing. I must be a bad, horrible thing. What guy has sex with you and doesn't come? Again, this wasn't a possibility in the stories I had heard about first sex. I was disappointed afterward, but not in the way I'd imagined.

We broke up a few weeks later. I don't know if the relationship had run its course or the sex was as depressing for him as it was for me. Later I heard that he told people we'd never done it. That it didn't *count*.

• • • • • •

The reason things ended was sadly dull: he stopped being in love with me. There wasn't anything wrong with me, he said. He thought I was beautiful and cool. The problem was that I was just one person. And he was young and the world was big and full of lots of other people.

After we broke up it took a while to disentangle ourselves. We had friends in common and we couldn't let go of the physical relationship, either. I missed hanging out with him, laughing with him. Finally, I had to cut it off completely for my sanity.

But when I was especially sad and missing him, the memory of that first sex wasn't what pulled me back. Though I didn't like how he phrased it, I knew what he meant when he said it didn't count.

Instead, the scene that made me feel his loss so keenly wasn't the *sex* at all. It was way back at the beginning of knowing him. Something that I didn't think would have *counted* in the first place.

• • • • • •

It is November, one of those days when the dark comes on so quick. We are in my house, nobody there but us. A rare intersection of space and time and privacy. We can act like adults. We don't have to sneak or worry.

So we drink cherry brandy. We talk about whatever. But we know talking is a waste of time, so we go up to my bedroom.

"Let's get naked," he says, which I think is so funny and wonderful! Because it's so honest. When someone suggests it this way—*Let's get naked!*—you can say *yes* or you can say *no*; there's no gray area, there's no language hiding intention.

This is how everything looks, then: We're both in my bed, tangled up together on top of the quilt. His jeans, T-shirt (white) and flannel shirt (blue) are tossed on the floor. His boxer shorts (white with green stripes) are pushed down a little. I'm in my bra (black satin) and my Levis are on the floor. My underwear are cotton bikinis, bought in a pack of six. My bed is a single and fits both of us, though his feet hang over the edge a bit. We're touching each other in places we've already touched (under the bra and boxers and undies) but because we're alone it feels gigantic and luxurious, like we're just discovering America.

Except, soon it's 9:26 PM, according to the clock on my night-stand. He's still sixteen and his parents expect him home by ten.

I straighten my bra, put on my shirt, get up to go pee. When I come back he's sitting on my bed, wearing his jeans, putting on his T-shirt. Seeing him dress is unbearably sad but I pull on my own jeans, resigned to our night together being over.

Then, as he's putting his flannel back on, even though he needs to get home, I kiss him again. Reach down to feel if he's hard.

He's always hard. I think that's magical.

I push his flannel off his shoulders. Wrench his T-shirt off. Kneel down between his knees.

We don't say anything.

We pull his jeans down around his ankles. He's in his striped boxers again, his white tube socks pulled up his calves in that dorky boy way.

My hands are on his thighs, touching the blond hairs there that I think are almost pretty, feeling how flat and strong his muscles are. There is nothing on my body like that. I am soft and smooshy despite my efforts to be fit and pretty. But he works very hard to be strong and fit and athletic. Harder than I am willing to, actually, but he thinks nothing of it. I'm almost jealous that his body is so unlike mine. But not quite jealous, because I am touching his body as if it were mine, and being together means I can have it whenever I want now, like it belongs to me.

From where I kneel, I don't worry what I look like. My hair covers my shoulders and chest and the workings of my face. My body folds beneath him, shadowed. I don't look up so I don't know if he is watching or just feeling what I'm doing.

We pull down his boxers and a second later I feel him in my mouth. Under my palms his thighs are trembling, but what I'm doing is solid and clear. Honest. I hear the sound of him sucking in his breath, then a sighing noise from deep in his chest. Every sound he makes tells me how it feels.

I feel everything too, and not just with my brain, which is reeling with excitement and a kind of crazed curiosity. Physically, I am right there with him. Feeling through his body how good it feels. Tasting everything, smelling everything. These aren't tastes or smells I can name but they're familiar. Like I should have known them. Like I'd always known them.

Like things that are private and exclusive.

Like being an adult: an acquired taste.

Sweet, salty, sour, bitter. The way his body tenses. The way he breathes, soft, then hard. It's perfect. It feels like something I'm creating, not just a thing that's happening.

When he comes, which is just a few minutes into it, I swallow it all—the sweet, salty, sour, bitter. All of it.

For a little while, neither of us move. I don't say a word, I don't even look at him. I press my hands on his thighs like I'm going to stand up.

That's when he scoops me up and holds me tighter than anyone ever has before and he says, "God, you're so great. I just love you so much."

Time stops in that moment. I am dizzy with victory and gratitude. The hallway light is on, the nightstand lamp is off. The bed and quilt, dark beneath us, and his thighs so strong, holding me on him, holding us both up as we press together. The words he's said between us. I don't say *I love you* back. I don't need to because I know that this is him thanking me. Spontaneously. The most genuine and vulnerable I've ever known a boy to be.

I've never made anyone happy like this. I've given him something that surprised him, and it surprised me as well: He liked it, he appreciated it, he made me feel valuable and precious. And competent, just as I am.

I've created a recipe to making his body feel good on the first try and I've witnessed the first time he enjoyed it. I know that I get to be in his memory forever. This also feels rare and lucky. Destined. Singular. Unreplaceable.

• • • • • • •

A blowjob. Sucking dick. Head.

You could say that it wasn't that noble.

You could say that I was feasting on a banquet of crumbs.

You could say, "Why didn't he get you off, Carrie?"

You could say all that and the grown woman I am now would nod along with you.

But this memory, this first time, is the one that I always return to. *God, you're so great.*

The clock is ticking, he needs to get home, this is ending, this is bad timing. But I don't regret it. I know so much lays before us.

I'm comfortable, for once, being myself. I'm thinking about how it feels to feel good. I'm thinking about sex and God and how bodies don't lie. How so many things I've believed about myself are false.

I just love you so much.

At this moment, sitting across his thighs, holding him tight, all I know is that I am valuable and good. And that no one, no girl before me, has ever made him feel this. And no matter what happens—the dark places we end up not visible or conceivable to me then as I perch on him full of happiness and delight—this is real, this is good. Because, here, in this moment, in this memory, I will always get to be the first one. And that is what counts.

Sex is everywhere in American culture.

The cover of Cosmopolitan tantalizes with "101 Tips to Satisfy Your Man in Bed." The Sport's Illustrated swimsuit issue bombards us with what a hot woman is supposed to look like. Pounding rap lyrics remind us that everyone is doing it—or should be. One Hollywood blockbuster after another depicts women going down and getting laid.

All that sex sure looks like fun—as long as you're straight.

Young women have always been the target of mixed messages about sex. From school sex education to religious messaging to public health advisories, we've heard that sex is dangerous, dirty, and off-limits. And if you're queer? The messages get worse: immoral, sinful, and illegal.

How do we make sense of it all? Do we aspire to look like Victoria's Secret models with come-hither smiles? Do we take so-called "purity" pledges? Do we suffocate our own desires?

Maybe the first step forward is to claim our bodies as our own.

In the next story, Sidney writes about surviving Catholic school and finding pleasure in sharing her own anatomy.

> It was the first time I had ever made someone moan. I felt **capable**, powerful.

> ... she **sweetly** kissed me again. I kissed her back, feeling less afraid.

> I **moaned** and moved against her, like a rhythmic tide with increasing rapidity.

3

Sharing My Anatomy

Sidney Joaquin-Vetromile

Novels were my first explorations of sex. In bookstores, I would pick up titles from the romance section, wander to a different, more neutral aisle (calendars, perhaps), and surreptitiously scan for certain key words to find the scenes I wanted.

Slick. Moan. Hands. Thrust.

The sex was always heterosexual. I never cared much for the characters' backstories but I liked reading about what a gentle, attentive lover might do to anatomy like mine.

One sex scene in a long-forgotten novel lingered with me. A young man, a mechanic, coupled with a slightly older woman in the back of a car he had been repairing. He had gotten hard and penetrated his lover but, this being his first time, he had come almost immediately. Paralyzed with shame, he began to pull out but she wrapped her legs around him and told him, gently, that he wasn't finished yet. She kept him inside her and then moved against him like a slow, insistent tide.

With the claiming of her own pleasure, her increasing wetness, her warmth, and her patience, the young man's desire and erection returned, stronger now. They came together, sweating and seizing each other in gratitude. She helped to banish his shame, replacing it with a new faith in his capacity for intimacy and the loving exchange of pleasure.

The book was told in the third person but in this scene I imagined myself as the young man—uncertain, filled with desire, prone to mistakes but guided to orgasm by someone who knew I had no reason to be ashamed. Guided to orgasm by a woman. Someone who shared my anatomy.

I was far too frightened to articulate this physical longing. The first time I made myself come as a teenager, with rhythmic thrusts against a pillow, I felt surprised and terrified. I prayed for forgiveness.

As a student at a conservative, all-girls Catholic school I absorbed many awful messages about sex. When I was fifteen, Proposition 22, an antigay marriage measure in California, was overwhelmingly voted into law. I asked my favorite teacher, a gentle, good-humored nun, how she voted. She launched into a vicious monologue. "Men have to use their penises and their mouths. They place their genitals in each other's anuses. Women have to use their fingers, or worse, other devices. It's unspeakable. It's morally wrong. It brings disease. I'm a Catholic sister. How do you think I voted?"

Unspeakable. Devices. Fingers.

The words echoed in my mind, disgusting me. Instinctively I sat on my hands, as if she had revealed me to the entire class.

The following year, my high school invited two women from the local district attorney's office to talk to us about sex crimes. Their main prosecuting concern was not sexual assault; it was sex among minors. The DA gave us dire warnings. Even if the participants were consenting and underage—both sixteen, for example—they could be charged as sex offenders. If one partner was eighteen and the other partner was younger, the older one would be charged as a

statutory rapist. Yes, they would pursue same-sex offenders. Digital
sex, they said, waggling their fingers in the air, was a crime too.

When the school hired a police officer to talk to us about sexual
assault, his advice was insane. "If you don't want to get raped, you
won't get raped. You have to really believe in yourself. And you have
to be willing to do crazy things. Poop your pants. Piss your pants.
That'll stop the rapist. He'll be too grossed out."

What did we learn? That sex outside of marriage would destroy
us. *Criminal. Broken. Unwholesome. Alone.* And what waited for me,
as a closeted gay kid, was worse. Perhaps even an early death.

• • • • • • •

Still, I felt a particular longing for intimacy and sex that grew each
year. I kept to my romance novels, finding new scenes. I learned
how to touch myself with my own hands, how to draw circles with
my fingers where my body liked it best, how to touch my clitoris
to come quickly, and how to make myself wait for a more intense,
drawn-out orgasm.

When chat rooms first came into vogue, I discovered cybersex. I
would ask faceless men to imagine what they wanted to do to me,
blocking the ones who wanted to be rough, clicking away from
the ones who wanted to receive oral sex. I chatted with the ones
who wanted to enter me with their tongues or penetrate me slowly
with one hand while touching my clitoris. These conversations
were strange, anonymous affirmations of my desire. At school I felt
humiliated. Online I felt powerful.

I avoided lesbian chat rooms. Participating there would mean there
was something irreversibly wrong with me. I could not allow myself
to imagine the sex I wanted to have. I told myself that cybersex,
fantasizing, and self-pleasuring were mere misdemeanors, preventing me from the felony of partnered sex. I would never have sex
with someone else. I would suppress real-life crush feelings. I would
stay in the safety of novels, internet chats, and my imagination.

Minor sins, not mortal ones.

But I *was* having crushes. My body was, against my will, teaching me what I liked. Women who were more athletic than I was. Women who ran track, played soccer, and stole bases in softball. Women whose navy, uniform cardigans clung precisely to their strong chests and arms. Women who wore their battered athletic sneakers off the field and told dirty jokes. Women who made everyone laugh. I liked messy hair and quick smiles and mischief. I liked the soft mounds above flat torsos.

I would look and then try not to look.

I would feel and then try not to feel.

Prohibition and pleasure and hope and self-hatred existed in the same heartbeat. There were so many voices in my head:

You are so beautiful.
Don't tell her that.
I want.
I'm disgusting.
God gave me up unto vile affections.
I want to give to you.
I want you to give to me.

But at night, after my solitary orgasms, I could sleep more easily. My heart and my mind would go quiet, comforted by my capable body.

· · · · · · ·

I met Maureen my senior year in high school. She was goofy and awkward, with her hair always in her face. She loved the musical *Rent*, which I'd never heard of, and would belt out lyrics in her car, offering to teach me how to sing.

I didn't have a crush on Maureen immediately. Mostly she confused me, collapsing, as she did, into mumbles and laughter whenever I was near her. I remember that I could sense when she was near. Maybe it was her perfume or shampoo or perhaps I could read her presence in the air like an olfactory prediction of what would pass between us.

In the middle of our senior year, Maureen found my chat name online. We began to talk every night. We told each other stories about school, our families, and what we wanted to do in the future. I began to sense we were skirting a subject but I couldn't imagine what it was.

Finally, at midnight, she said over chat that she liked me. She had a crush on me that she had been trying to suppress.

I called her on her phone immediately.

"I'm hiding under my desk now," she said, by way of greeting me.

"What? I can't believe this!" I said happily.

"You couldn't tell?" Maureen asked.

"No way! Not at all!" I said.

I had been, in the language of my Filipina mother, *torpe*—so dense, so locked up in my own anxiety, that I noticed none of the cues until Maureen told me directly.

Torpe.

"So," I said, all suave (as in, not suave at all). "Um. What do we do?"

"I don't know," Maureen said honestly.

Maureen and I were shy with each other at school in the following weeks. Suddenly, we were both mumbling and laughing awkwardly. Every day we broke away from our broader circle of friends to be alone together.

She invited me to an Ani DiFranco concert. We drove an hour to the venue, far from our conservative town, and pressed shoulders together through the whole show. We saw older women kissing and pressing their bodies together. When Maureen dropped me off at home, we pressed foreheads together, and she waited for me to look at her, but I couldn't. She told me to go inside, worried I was getting cold.

We didn't kiss until a week after the concert. She slept over at my house, and we locked the door as soon as my mom fell asleep. Maureen and I kissed once. Then I soon went to sleep, guilty and panicked, too scared to do more. Later, I woke up in Maureen's arms and settled into her, welcoming her warm, new presence.

In the morning, when we woke up next to each other, I said, "Wow, revelation! No matter what happens in the future, that will always belong to you. My first kiss." In response, she sweetly kissed me again. I kissed her back, feeling less afraid.

• • • • • • •

Over the next few weeks, we went slowly. She was also attracted to boys and had more experience with kissing than I did, but she didn't rush me. I was so terrified by the district attorney's lecture that I insisted on waiting until Maureen was eighteen before I would touch her below her waist.

One night, when we were making out, we kissed more intensely than usual, for nearly an hour. We shifted together on my bed, and her knee softly found the warmth between my legs. I pressed against her, enjoying the new contact. She gripped my breasts and found my rising nipples. I moaned and moved against her, like a rhythmic tide with increasing rapidity. It arrived before I knew it was happening—my orgasm. I came for the first time with another person, with someone who cared about me.

With a woman.

I opened my eyes and clung to her shoulders, my relief mingling with the old shame.

"I don't know if we should do that again," I said.

"Okay," Maureen said gently.

But I thought about it later. The moment of my orgasm, the feel of her fingertips finding my nipples, the firm heat of her knee against the part of me where I felt pleasure the most. I did not feel broken when it happened. I felt whole. I felt happy.

We tried again a few weeks later, after Maureen's birthday when we were finally the same age. This time, we slept over at her parents' house.

She started slow with her palms along my torso. My skin there shook with hope and fear, unused to the presence of another person. She asked me if I was ready, and I nodded. She touched me where I had only ever touched myself. She touched me differently, gently drawing her fingers from the wetness of my vagina to the swelling near my clitoris. I made small, involuntary sounds of gratitude and approval.

I touched her with my hands too. She felt like me: warm at first, and then, as I slowly moved my fingers, she turned slick, damp. I traced circles near the top of her vulva where I thought her clitoris might be, the way I liked to touch myself. She moaned. It was the first time I had ever made someone moan. I felt capable, powerful.

I felt like smiling.

So I kissed her and I smiled while I did. I learned what it was to kiss someone and find her mouth cold from the way she had been gasping with desire.

She smiled against my smiling mouth.

Years later, Maureen and I would break up and reconcile more than once. I would watch her date boys and feel a terrible, jealous sorrow. Years after that, our friendship would resume, and she would invite me to her wedding to a kind and funny man, our mutual friend. She would be open about her first relationship having been with a woman. I would always be grateful to her for helping to banish my shame and for helping me to learn my capacity for intimacy.

· · · · · · ·

Over the years I would learn and relearn a different kind of revelation. I would learn to whom I really belonged. I was not owned by a church's cruel teachings. I was not owned by condemnation, isolation, or fear. It did not matter what the state, my school, a religion, or a teacher claimed. I belonged to me. My body was my own, with all of its capacity for pleasure, healing, and wholeness. I could share my body with someone who shared my anatomy. I could share my heart with a woman who would protect it.

I belonged to me.

The first time is going to be amazing—right? Sure, it might hurt a little at first but then . . . ah! We've watched romantic comedies. It's going to be all glitter and roses. We've seen porn. Sexy-hot-lusty-busty fun is there for the taking.

Besides, everyone is doing it—aren't they?

Actually, they aren't.

At age seventeen, less than 50 percent of young women have had sex. By age twenty, that increases to about 75 percent. Most of those are having sex with a steady partner.[1]

But there is lot of pressure to get down to business, and it can be tough territory to navigate—especially if you're convinced that ecstasy is only a thrust away!

4
The First Rule of College
Kiersi Burkhart

My virginity was like an uncomfortable but fashionable little black dress.

It blistered and chafed me, and more than anything I wanted to throw it in a tin garbage bin and reduce it to smoldering ashes—but not until after everyone had gotten a good eyeful of me wearing it.

I still don't understand why I wanted it gone so badly. Why was I so ready to slough it off on the nearest passerby, like some conspicuous dandruff? Isn't virginity supposed to be treasured? Shouldn't I have grasped it tightly and carefully until only the worthiest partner came along?

But the idea of sex had been pumped up to colossal size in my head. I fantasized about how incredible my first good fuck would be, how my whole life had been leading up to that one magical (oh, and it *would* be magical) moment. All I wanted was to get that teensy little uncomfortable bit of virginity over and done with as quickly as possible and get on to the fun part.

And can anyone blame me for not having a clue? In my favorite fantasy novels, after that first awful moment, the heroine's first time is soul-crushingly fulfilling. In sex ed, it was boiled down to a diagram of a hymen that uncomfortably resembled a hagfish's mouth. My folks believed in *no sex before marriage*, so they weren't much help. And talking to older girls? One I knew said she hadn't felt anything, but her sister piped up, "Of course not. It's always easier for fat girls. Like throwing a hot dog down a wet hallway." (Later, in tears, the first sister confessed that she'd started early with sex toys and that more likely than not she could thank a blue silicon cock for her painless first time.)

I knew, simply *knew*, based on my extensive research, the pleasure would improve after that first time. Sex would become mind-blowing. Weren't the internet porn actresses always moaning with pure glee? They'd pant and scream and eventually, after some thorough pillaging, come so hard that their bodies shook like twigs in a rainstorm. Wasn't that also waiting for me?

This obsession with sex sunk its claws into me at eleven years old. Soon it completely took over, and it would keep digging in for another five years. After all that time dreaming and fantasizing and clicking through internet ads of huge black cocks, I wanted my first time over and done. I was ready to move on with my life—my real, grown-up, adult life, where sex was as normal as weekend brunch.

But that godforsaken *dress*. I was still wearing it, and as long as I lived under my parents' roof, their hawk-eyes watching me, no one was likely to get in and peel it off me anytime soon. So I vowed to myself: get to college, rip the dress off as quickly as possible, and get on with the good stuff.

Now, as I learned it, the first rule of college is this: *no hall-cest*. (Followed closely by *cover your smoke alarm with plastic wrap if you want to smoke a joint in your room* and *never eat the cubed ham at the salad bar after 6 PM*.) Do not—whatever you do—*do not* sleep with your hall mates. You can sleep with the guy on first floor if you're on third floor, or better yet, the shaggy fellow you sometimes spot

in the dorm across the picnic area, but woe betide you if you sleep
with the hunky, blond football player who lives in 303.

But it was an unofficial rule.

So when I met said hunky, blond football player living down
the hall, I might as well have placed a bull's-eye on his crotch and
taken out my sniper rifle. He was easy prey: horny, college-aged,
and not the brightest crayon in the box. Manipulating Vince into
fucking me was like covering a toddler's eyes and convincing him
you were no longer there.

"Don't do it," my roommate told me. "Hall-cest. Ten foot pole.
Also, free condoms on the RA's door, but seriously—*don't do it.*"

At that point, it didn't matter. The dress was cinched so tight I
couldn't breathe. I was out of high school, on my own, and there
was no point wearing it where my parents couldn't see me.

So I made remarks to Vince in the coed bathroom about how
much I needed to get laid. How relationships were boring, how I
hated clingy girls—all that porno stuff I thought boys wanted to
hear. We kissed late one night walking through the rose garden
and fooled around under the flag pole. Coming home early from
class one afternoon, we were the only two people in the hall. I
asked him to come over and help me move my desk. In a meager
minute, we were naked on my beanbag chair.

I never told him I was a virgin. He seemed happy to assume I
wasn't. I was happy to let him assume.

He scrambled for the purple condom shoved in his wallet and
remarked on my bush. He'd never fucked a girl with a full one
before, he said, not hiding his distaste all that well.

Not once would I forget to shave after that remark. For six years
I carefully manicured the topiary of my pubic hair—airstrips,
arrows, boxes, triangles, all neatly trimmed, the smoothness of my
lips maintained daily—until a far better man told me I should do
whatever the hell I wanted with my own naturally occurring hair.

When the condom wrapper finally tore, that sudden panic one
must feel right before skydiving or bungee jumping set in, and

I began to wonder if maybe I should back out. Maybe I wasn't actually ready to take off the dress yet. Didn't it look good on me? Didn't it make my parents happy? Didn't I want somebody *better*?

But Vince was already shrink-wrapping himself in neon purple latex. Before the panic could worm its way into action, he pushed in. I wouldn't realize until later that even the most novice penis around will at least give you a little foreplay to lube you up and jazz your jets.

But I guess you get what you pay for.

The pain wasn't horrible, which surprised me. I'd imagined it sharp and twisting, like a knife, when it was far more like a doctor pinching the flesh of your arm and shooting you full of some nameless vaccine. Everything hurt for a moment, then faded to a dull ache as Vince pumped away. He didn't seem to notice the just-swallowed-a-warhead look on my face or seem perturbed at all that I was a prone, unenthusiastic participant—which wasn't particularly my fault, considering I couldn't feel anything besides *pump, pump, pump* and *ache, ache, ache*.

Maybe he did notice and he just didn't care.

After what felt like a minute, maybe two if I am being generous, a ghost of a tingle somewhere down inside me started creeping upward. A tangle of ivy wove its way from my uterus to my hips to my collar bones.

Oh! Was that it? Was that a shadow of the thing that made porn stars scream? It was, though, only a sad fraction of what I could do for myself on my own time.

Before it could grow into anything more than an ephemeral hint of pleasure, Vince's slippery purple cock popped free like a slug escaping a Chinese finger trap.

The condom had slipped perilously close to his tip, the cream-filled latex dangling down. I made a sad little sound and reached for him again, as if more *pump, pump, ache* could actually bring that wary tingle to the surface. But he pushed me away, peeling off the condom that smelled faintly of spoiled grapes, and said, "I'm done anyway."

I lay sprawled on the beanbag, too shocked to move, or object, or even scowl at him. Vince climbed to his feet, pulled on his boxers and jeans, slipped his shirt over his head and said, "See you."

Then he was gone. The moron didn't even close the door behind him.

I got up, slammed the door shut, and slumped against it. I'd burned the dress, all right. I could almost taste the acrid tang of seared polyester.

Maybe it wasn't the smell of my thrown-away virginity. Maybe it was the smell of shame. Or disappointment.

Or reality.

The little black dress had been replaced by something else but I couldn't pinpoint what. I wasn't naked and free, a peaceful hippie in a sweat lodge, like I'd expected. Like I'd hoped.

Looking around my room, nothing appeared to have changed except some new rumples in the beanbag cover. I felt like that beanbag—used, left with a few crinkles, but otherwise completely the same.

I'd been nothing but a toy for some douche bag down the hall. That was the part that struck me most, the part that made me stand there, staring at the beanbag, unwilling to move. Was I getting as good as I got for wanting to make a toy out of him too? I didn't feel any better now that the dress was gone—all I'd acquired was a throbbing ache between my legs.

I hadn't magically become a grown, adult woman. I especially had not become a moaning Barbie in a porno.

I'd been a cheap thrill. And that was it.

For weeks I hid from people on my hall, people who might guess. I told none of my friends about it, like a victim after a con, when all the money she'd put in a sure scheme vanishes in a puff of engine exhaust.

I'd been tricked by porn into thinking some sort of instant magic was hidden inside a hunky dude's dick. But everyone had been lying to me. Sex wasn't pleasurable for women—Vince had taught me that much, at least.

And the discovery that movie sex and real sex lay galaxies apart set me into full, Kill Bill–style retribution mode.

I had ten partners in one year.

But it was far more about the game and less about the enjoyment. I accepted sex as it really was for me: a fun sport, a game of pick-up soccer, that distant hint of pleasure always lingering right outside my grasp.

I assumed it would always be that way.

• • • • • •

They say in sex ed that virginity only happens one time. That once you break your hagfish-shaped hymen, that's it.

You're deflowered.

You're officially in the club.

But it's just not fucking true.

Life is an endless roller coaster of first times, of lost virginities. My first time having *great* sex was like taking that dress off all over again—slower, sweeter, better. It captured me completely by surprise. He was older, wiser, a little handsomer; he knew his way around me like he'd drawn the map himself.

After that, sex wasn't just a sport anymore, where the satisfaction comes from finishing tired and muddy and as roughed-up as possible to show off your battle scars to your friends. This new sex was full and thick and wonderful. It was noisy and honest. Sometimes wild and sometimes slow. This sex was filled with every kind of feeling my body and soul were capable of having.

There will always be more first times.

Even if it feels like everyone you know is having sex there can be lots of good reasons to wait. According to a survey of inexperienced young people reported by the Guttmacher Institute in 2014, the three most common reasons they gave for abstaining were religious and moral convictions, fear of pregnancy, and waiting for the right person.

There's no shame in waiting. You can wait until you feel ready. You can wait until you really know what having sex will mean to you. You can wait for a partner you love and trust.

In the next story, Karen tells us about her wedding night and why she waited.

5

It's a Nice Day for a White Wedding

Karen Jensen

The music started.

Everyone stood.

I was twenty-two and getting married.

As I walked down the aisle, my head swiveled from left to right. All I could think was *everyone knows*. At the end of the aisle stood this man that I was going to marry. He was dressed up in a tuxedo, grinning at me, slightly nervous. And all I could think was *everyone knows we're going to have sex tonight*.

Earlier that day a not-so-tactful member of my family got a glimpse of me in my wedding gown and tried to crack a joke. "Yeah, like you deserve to wear white." It came off as mean because I knew he was trying to make a dig about my faith, but the thing is, if you consider what the white gown used to signify, I really did deserve to wear it. My soon-to-be husband and I had been together for three and a half years, engaged for two and a half of them, and I was still, in every technical sense of the word, a virgin.

As a teenager, I feared sex. Not sex in itself, but the consequences of sex. I had big plans: going to college, becoming self-sufficient, rubbing my success in the face of every asshat in my family who thought I would never amount to anything.

I had seen my mom divorce my dad and try to put the pieces of her life back together. I wanted to make sure that I had a strong foundation to take care of myself and be an independent woman. A baby would have derailed all of that. Besides, getting pregnant as a teenager would have proved the asshats right, and I just didn't have the stomach for that.

I had places to go, things to say, and a world to change.

Plus, somewhere along the way I had become a Christian. I had always been a romantic, a believer in soul mates and true love, so the Christian idea of the sacrament of marriage and fidelity fit right along with my belief system. My grandparents and the way they had grown old together were the perfect ideal, an example of true love to rival even the greatest of love stories. Forget Romeo and Juliet—they died. My inspiration came from these two old souls who had become my bedrock of stability in a world that held constant chaos and change. I wanted what they had for myself.

For all these reasons, I was a virgin on the day I walked down that aisle to my future husband. Vows were exchanged. Songs sung. Cake eaten. And then I threw the bouquet and we ran.

It was late when we arrived at the little lakeside cottage for our honeymoon. We had almost missed the last boat across the lake. We were tired. We were overwhelmed. We turned on the TV.

What can I say? Three and a half years with no sex and you kind of develop a pattern.

The weather turned bad. The sky grew dark and ominous. Rain pelted the roof. Before long, a storm raged outside. The wind whipped violently through the air, making the house shake and shudder and groan. The lights flickered. They flashed. And then they went out, plunging us into darkness. We sat in silent darkness for a few moments, uncertain. Hesitant.

"What do we do now?" he asked.

A lightbulb went on in my head. I knew. I knew that we could finally do what we had waited for all this time.

So I pounced.

In the unsexiest way possible, I pounced on my new husband.

I flung myself at him with a mixture of glee—*Yes, finally I'm having sex!*—and trepidation—*Oh crap, I'm having sex. How do I do this? Kissing! You start with kissing, right?* Like a jungle cat, I was suddenly there in the dark trying to kiss his lips. Except I don't have jungle cat vision, so my first kiss landed on his nose. We banged heads. We fumbled in the dark, trying to make our way—still kissing, of course—into the bedroom.

That's where the magic would happen. I knew this because I'd seen it time and time again in every romantic movie I'd ever seen. And then there was all this weird, awkward dancing. Trying to remove clothes. Trying to find each other in the dark. Trying to figure out exactly how you could insert *Tab A* into *Slot B*. I knew the mechanics of sex in the same way I technically knew how to change a flat tire. But I had never done either and knowing, it turns out, is not the same as actually doing.

It was the exact opposite of romantic.

There was, in fact, laughing. Limbs got tangled. Neither of us walked away from that first experience feeling like a red-hot sex machine. It was nothing like what I had grown up seeing in the movies. The movies, it turned out, had lied. But it *was* fun. It was fulfilling. It was, in fact, quite amazing. It felt like more than love, this trust and surrender that I had just given to the man with whom I had sworn to share my life.

When we were done, I stood up, dizzy with excitement and really needing to pee, but as soon as I did, all of this stuff came gushing out of me. I was appalled and a little grossed out. When I mentioned it, this newly crowned husband of mine asked, "Well, what did you think happened with it all?"

The truth is, I had never thought about it, but then no one had explained this moment to me. There is so much no one tells you about sex, including the fact that it can be slimy.

The Mr. and I have been married for a while now, and we have gotten better at the whole sex thing. Sometimes it is sexy, though more often it's still funny. Sometimes we still bang heads. Sometimes I go in for the dramatic kiss in the dark and find that I am nowhere near my target and am, in fact, kissing his nose.

We have two kids so I'm pretty sure people realize that we have sex, but it turns out no one really thinks about it. And they weren't that day I walked down the aisle either. Looking back, I'm pretty sure they were just thinking about how I was the most beautiful bride ever—right?

Sexual autonomy.

It's not a sexy phrase but it's a good one. It means that you get to choose what you do. You're in charge—every kiss, every stroke, every time you rip your panties off, or don't.

It's all you.

This is a book about first times. Consensual first times. Chosen first times.

When you don't choose and sexual things happen anyway, that's not sex. It's violence. An unwelcome kiss. A hand grabbing your ass. Coerced oral sex. Rape. If you don't want it to happen, it's assault. (And if this has happened to you, I urge you to report the crime and visit RAINN.org, a support organization for survivors.)

Just as sex can make us powerful, it can also make us vulnerable, naked in every sense of the word. This is especially true for survivors of sexual abuse. Some respond by choosing abstinence because it is so difficult to contemplate letting anyone touch their bodies again. Others respond to violated boundaries by giving up on boundaries altogether. Sometimes flashbacks of abuse accompany their consensual sexual experiences for years.

For survivors, reclaiming their sexual selves can be a long road. In the next story, Christa lets us walk beside her for a while.

6

I Would Have a Heart

Christa Desir

I was six years old the first time a man put his hands on me sexually. It wasn't the first time I'd been exposed to the idea of sex, but it was the first time I was a participant. Exposure to trauma at such a young age left little room for the milestones of "firsts." As a teenager I did not care about rounding bases or giving up my V card, I cared about trying to fill the part of me that had been taken away, the part of me that was unprotected. I cared about being wanted, as if that could provide protection. And sex became a means to an end, a way to feel wanted.

I became the girl who would give a guy a blow job in a living room with people walking in and out to get their coats. The girl who gave a guy a hand job underneath a thin blanket on the lawn of a completely packed outdoor concert. I became the thing people wanted more than anything else, if only for a few minutes.

I wanted to be wanted with the voraciousness that addicts approach a fix. But after years of multiple hookups, male and female, I still had no balm for my many broken parts. At nineteen years old, I had no notion of what love looked like.

I decided to get away from everything and everyone. I would spend the summer after my sophomore year of college on Block Island, a small island off the coast of Rhode Island. I had a plane ticket with a return date at the end of the summer, eighty dollars in my pocket, and a tent to sleep in. I was alone because the friend who was supposed to spend the summer with me backed out at the last minute. I had no job and no real plan. But I was stubborn and determined to prove that I was fucking fine and could take care of myself no matter what.

The first thing I saw when I stepped off the ferry was a giant sign that said, "Absolutely no camping on the island." Twenty thousand tourists descend on Block Island every summer, and the few year-round residents wanted to discourage drifters like me. So I found the police station and pitched my tent in the woods about fifty feet behind it. I had something to prove, after all.

Within two hours of setting up camp I landed a job as a cashier at Bella Pizza. I talked the owner into hiring me like I did everything else. I made him think I was invaluable to the sale of his pizza. It was a strange sort of bravado I carried inside. And one I had with men much more than women. Men were easy. In my mind, all I had to do was make them feel like they were the most important person in the room and that I was lucky to be around them.

My first night on the island I was sitting at the pizza parlor chatting up my new manager about housing options when he introduced me to some employees from the nearby hotel, including a gorgeous waiter named Brian. He was one of those tall, lean boys who wore close-shaved blond hair and a smirk. He was nineteen, had a deep golden tan, and smoked Marlboro Lights between his thumb and forefinger—the guy way. Sexy as hell when you put the whole package together.

In spite of my girlfriend back at college who had sent me to the island with a book of Sappho's poetry and long, wet, good-bye kisses, the sight of that smirk awoke the voracious and desperate she-demon inside me. I wanted to make him crave me.

So I did what I always did, I played to my strengths, or at least what I assumed my strengths were to guys. Mostly, I knew how to give good blow jobs. I had a really big mouth, and I swallowed. Surely these made me worthy of being craved. Because what guy doesn't want sexual services from a girl who swallows?

I dangled fat, sexual innuendos in Brian's face. He didn't blink. I did the cherry stem trick with my tongue. He didn't fall for it. I hung on his every word and made him feel important. He lit another cigarette and waited. Brian waited all that first night. He waited for days. He was waiting for me to become me.

At first, I was certain he'd decided I was only friend material. But he spent every free minute at the pizza place. He let me talk. He asked questions. He batted my efforts at seduction away and clung to the other parts of me, the big brain and the thoughtful reader and the girl who told funny stories about all the stupid shit she'd done. He dribbled out little pieces of himself that I snatched up and cherished. He kissed me, he held my hand, and then he walked me back to my tent every night. Brian hadn't friend-zoned me, but he wasn't fucking me either. This was different.

Two weeks in, I decided he wasn't sexual. I wondered if he was smoking pot or drinking a lot. I'd heard those things could cause a guy's sex drive to wither. The fact that Brian had spent so much time getting to know me and very little time being sexual with me had me convinced that he wasn't quite right.

I tested him. I told him of my now ex-girlfriend (who I'd written to break up with on day eight of island living), of my checkered past, of being a sexual violence survivor. I recounted the number of blow jobs I'd given to guys I barely knew. I pushed him as hard as I could. I poured myself out and set it at his feet and waited to see if he would spit on it or reject it, but nothing seemed to talk him out of me.

His want was so different than what I'd ever known.

"Do you want to stay the night in the tent?" I finally asked him on the fifteenth day.

"No," he said. "It's starting to smell in there and I'm working in the morning, but I'll see you after."

I slipped my hand in the waistband of his jeans and he inched back. "Don't you worry about the cops?" he asked.

"Not really. What are they going to do?"

He kissed me then, and it tasted like cigarettes, mine and his, and I pressed myself against him. But he didn't press back. He never did. Always so soft and gentle. Even half hard, like he was when I rubbed against him. He never asked for anything.

And day by day, my desire to make him want me sexually dulled. Being with Brian was a strange sort of reprieve. Every day would start with me holding my breath, waiting for him to decide I wasn't worth the trouble. But he didn't. He wanted to know me completely. He treated me like a gift, a whole person who fascinated him. No one had ever cared for me like that.

And I loved him for it. Deeply.

As the weeks passed, we slowly became more physical. It was almost inevitable with the way I pushed, but the way I desired him felt different—not clingy and voracious but new. Like this was a real milestone, a first I'd never even considered.

So one morning in the middle of the summer—before I had to work, before he had to work, when he came to see me because now we were desperate to see each other as much as we could, fighting against the inevitability of summer's end—I pulled him into my tent.

"Please," I said and slipped off his shirt, tugging at him, unbuttoning the top of his khaki shorts.

Morning sun streamed through the green walls of my illegal tent behind the police station. The light illuminated the planes of his chest, his flat stomach, his beautiful jawline. I almost couldn't believe what I was doing. It wasn't furtive or dark, shadowy to hide my dimpled thighs. I wasn't trying to get it over with. I wanted this moment to be different than how I'd always been.

I undid his zipper while he unbuttoned the front of my sundress. When we were both naked, I covered myself with my hands, squeezed my eyes tight, and waited to be found lacking for my doughy body.

He kissed my eyelids and whispered, "Hey, open up. Let me in."

I opened my eyes.

He trailed his tongue along my neck. His hands moved over me, and I tried to move them away, covering myself again.

"My stomach, my thighs," I choked out.

"Your skin is beautiful," he whispered.

Everything uncoiled. I dropped my hands and let him lick and touch. But the clawing feeling started up again, a different kind of anxiety now. I felt myself growing desperate, unhinged by the unknown. I had to get back in control. Sexual services—that's what I was good at. So I slid down his body, lower, almost past his stomach. My mouth ready to open and swallow.

He stopped me.

"You don't want me to?"

He shook his head. "I want to be with you. Not like that."

Because he knew what blow jobs meant to me—or didn't mean. A blow job was easily given away. He wanted connection, not servicing.

Now I had nothing to hide behind. I was an onion, the layers peeled back under his fingers to get to the heart. I was paralyzed with worry that he'd find no heart at all, that when he'd peeled everything back he'd just have smelly hands and tears and air.

He moved over me in this soft and patient way. He got hard and pressed against my thigh but still only touched me. If I reached for him, he batted my hands away.

I loved watching how his hands skimmed over me, even though I couldn't feel it—not the physical part of it—I was too numb still, too empty from years of unkind touch. Yet I loved seeing the trails of his gentle fingers because it felt like worship.

He fitted himself between my legs and it was easy and slow and like no sex I'd ever had. It didn't hurt. It wasn't rough or hard or deep. I was wet and it was an easy fit and I arched my hips because it made him grunt in this way that I liked. And I listened to us slapping together and it didn't feel like anything at all.

He came and I didn't because my heart and mind weren't connected to my body. My body was incapable of registering touch that wasn't pain. But my heart was so full of him. And afterward, maybe ten minutes later, he curled into me and the cool air from the tent door plus the mingled sweat on my skin made goose bumps pop up.

"I love you," he said. And he meant this. I understood it and knew that it had nothing to do with sex and everything to do with whatever he saw in me.

"I love you back."

He used his shirt to clean the cum from my inner thighs. We went outside to smoke cigarettes and walked to the pizza place for coffee, holding hands.

I thought, *This is what happy feels like.* It was a better high than being wanted. It was better than anything because I didn't think I deserved it but he made me feel like I did.

Soon after we had sex the first time, I rolled up my tent and moved into the employee housing where Brian lived. Think of overly crowded freshman dorm rooms and you've got a pretty good idea how it worked. The rooms were crapholes at best. Never cleaned. Dark and dank and hot as hell. We had sex in a single bunk with Brian's roommate, a barbecue chef at the hotel, snoring twenty feet away from us. It didn't matter. I could be quiet as a mouse having sex.

Because I hadn't found my voice.

I couldn't ask him to go down on me, though he would have gladly. I always stopped him before he even got close.

I didn't have orgasms, though his made me happy.

And I never asked him to use protection.

After sex, we'd hold hands and smoke cigarettes. Cum would leak onto my underwear and I'd hope I wasn't pregnant.

I never had one conversation with Brian about condoms. I'm sure he thought I was on the pill, but I was not. I was so seemingly in charge of myself sexually, so brazenly confident in what I'd done and who I'd done it with that he no doubt assumed I would never risk pregnancy. He didn't understand how, for so long, being wanted overrode risk. I wrote my best friend that I was practicing lunar-ception, hoping my cycles lined up with the moon and avoiding sex when the moon was waxing and I was ovulating. My best friend wrote back that I was a lunatic and needed to get my shit together.

So I spent the summer in this strange place of being deeply loved and still not safe.

I loved and Brian loved, but it wasn't perfect. Because he had to dig through so many layers of me. I think he kept waiting for my voice to come out, wanting me to be the same person in bed as I was in other parts of my life. But I didn't have it in me. Not yet. I handed him what I could because I loved him. And the sweet man did the best he could with my broken bits, sealing them together with saliva and cum and booze and smoke.

That's the thing about spending so much of one's life unprotected. You lose the ability to ask for protection anymore. You accept brokenness, and even if you search for healing you forget that when someone cements you back together you can still be broken again. I didn't need glue. I needed to be crack-proofed. I needed to coat myself in a seal so that if anyone dropped me I wouldn't break. But I wasn't thinking about that at age nineteen.

Brian was my first great love. He bridged a barrier within me. He added a new dimension to relationships that made me hope for more. He was imperfect and wonderful, all at the same time. He could not protect me, of course, but he showed me I was worthy of having my own voice, even if I couldn't find it with him.

Our relationship peeled away enough layers for me to know that when I got to the middle, I would have a heart. That was enough for me to begin the search for myself. To pursue a different kind of want, a better kind, the kind that would make me whole. Along the way, I found a voice to tell this story.

So often, first-time sex is laced with awkwardness. Where do I put my hands? Is my breath bad? How do all these bits line up?

Beyond the body and under our skin is the complicated rest of us, the wanting-wondering-worrying self. Does she want to kiss me there? Will he stop loving me? Am I okay?

But the thing about sex is that we are not alone.

That person—

The one there on the bed beside you—

The one you're planning to have sex with—

The two of you are in this together.

All those questions and worries are things you can talk about. In fact, once you and your partner start talking about what you want and why you want it, you might be surprised how sexy and powerful words can be.

{ . . . our bodies **twisted** to meet each other . . . . }

{ Her whole body
was warm and
familiar. }

{ . . . each swipe of her tongue
deepened my excitement. }

7
The Lion Poet
Laurel Isaac

The first night at writing camp I answered my dorm room door wearing boxers and a half-pulled-on T-shirt with the word *QUEER* in large letters. A counselor held out an Ethernet cord.

"Tech said you wanted one of these?" She eyed my laptop on the bed and my state of dress (or undress). I explained that I'd already found another cord. A slight tension hung in the air. Probably she knew I'd been masturbating.

The program director had already given us the *hands in pants* rule. "While at the Young Writers' Retreat, you can put your hands in your own pants but no one else's."

So, fuck, I was following protocol. Not that I needed guidance.

"Thanks anyway," I said. "I got the connection working on my own."

I met Scott the next day. He was a seventeen-year-old aspiring novelist from out West. Very white and serious looking with dark glasses and scruff on his face. We became friends in that way you sometimes do with the first person you meet in an unfamiliar place. A college campus in Massachusetts was certainly unfamiliar to both of us.

Scott towered over my fifteen-year-old self, but I felt relaxed with him. I told him he looked like Jonathan Franzen, which he liked. For the next two weeks, we sat together at every meal.

During the day, Scott and I wrote and critiqued drafts in different workshops. Mine was taught by a friendly nature writer named Wally who liked to have us journal without pause, the less time between pen and paper the better.

"If you get stuck, just write any words down," he said.

My journal was filled with sudden references to *sex, awkwardness,* and *being the worst writer.*

On weekends, the program offered outings to the lake or the cramped bookstore downtown. You had to sign up after breakfast on Saturday. There was always a long line. By the second Saturday, I felt at home enough to wait sprawled out on the grass outside. Two girls sat down near me, complaining about the wait.

"Where do you want go?" I asked.

"Bookstore."

"Same."

They were the first girls I'd really spoken to at the retreat. I always found it easier to talk to boys. But they seemed cool. I noticed the one with short red hair had a rainbow bracelet around her wrist. My heart leapt.

"Is that bracelet about pride?" I asked softly.

"Yeah, I'm gay."

"Cool. Me too," I beamed.

"I'm bi," the other girl said.

"Awesome!" said the redhead, grinning.

We introduced ourselves. Meghan, the red-haired one, was a playwright, and Maya, who had long dark hair, was a poet. We checked each other out. Though I could rattle off the names of dozens of queer authors, I'd never met a queer person my age.

"Are you out at school?" I asked.

"Duh." Meghan pulled up her shirt to reveal a rainbow belt.

"Kind of," Maya said. "They're assholes, so it doesn't matter. I'm out to my dad and brother."

The line for sign-ups disappeared but we stayed talking on the grass. Eventually Meghan jumped up to catch the bus into town. She had to get her mom a birthday present.

I lay next to Maya, looking up at the sky. It was hot. The quad cleared out. She looked seriously alternative but in a welcoming way.

"Where are you staying?" she asked, snapping a stick between her fingers.

"Fourth floor."

"Third. Who's your roommate?"

"I don't have one."

"Really?" She looked surprised.

"Yeah, I didn't know other people did."

She looked over at me. "Can I see yours?"

We wiped the grass off our backs and climbed the stairs to my floor. I unlocked the door with the key around my neck. Maya flopped down on my bed and I shut the door, putting the key on the table. The room was air-conditioned and dim. The walls were bare. It didn't look much different from when I moved in. I sat at my desk chair and watched her curl over on the narrow bed to look at me.

She really was a poet. As we talked more, Maya's speech took on a startling cadence and structure.

"It's like how, paws fast, words bash like a lion," she explained.

It was exciting and discordant. She was gorgeous and, in contrast to my emergent butchness, assertively feminine. At fifteen, she looked like an older woman, the kind I didn't think I'd get to hang out with. Hours passed. At one point she got quiet.

"What?" I asked.

"Nothing."

"No, tell me," I pleaded.

"I'm thinking something I shouldn't . . . I want to kiss you."

My chest tightened. I couldn't believe this was happening.

"No, that's good," I said in a rush, afraid she'd change her mind. "I mean . . . me too."

I smiled blankly, uncertain what came next. I'd never kissed anyone before. "Um . . . I'm not really looking for a girlfriend," I said, worried that this lion poet might be more than I could handle.

"Yeah, yeah, of course." She waved my protest away with one hand like dating was for other people.

I walked over to the bed, trying to mask my self-consciousness by playing it up. I tensed my shoulders, lumbered over to her, and plopped awkwardly onto the bed. I rolled my eyes as if to say, "Isn't this awkward? Kisses are the worst."

Then she kissed me.

Maya swiftly slipped her tongue inside my mouth and caressed mine in waves. Forget about playing it cool. I was beside myself. My clit leapt into awareness, jolted with feeling. I could feel wetness seeping into my underwear. Maya's mouth felt mind-bogglingly appealing. Her whole body was warm and familiar.

Sitting upright, our bodies twisted to meet each other, I was astonished by my arousal. It was like I'd discovered there was a second clit in my mouth, the way each swipe of her tongue deepened my excitement. Before, I'd sometimes worried that I wouldn't be able to orgasm with someone else touching me or that I would take too long and they'd get bored. I realized that if Maya were to touch me now, I'd come almost immediately.

I experimented with a firmer kiss, proud that I seemed to have gotten the hang of what to do with my mouth so quickly. Maya ran her soft fingers over my neck and up into my hair, pulling me closer. I felt lightheaded, hungry and satisfied at the same time. In the back of my mind I felt a shudder of pleasure as I thought, "Wow, I really am gay."

We made out a lot over the next few days. During breaks between workshops we'd head up to my room. At night we'd walk through the distant parts of campus holding hands while Maya made up poems about the trees. Once we passed the director who had explained the *hands in pants* rule and we separated quickly. But we hadn't actually gotten into each other's pants yet. I had no idea how that might happen.

One evening, the whole retreat was gathering to listen to a local author. I arrived early to a half-empty lecture hall. Scott, my old companion, slipped into a seat beside me.

"Hey, I haven't seen you in forever," I said, happy to see him. I'd missed his solid, rumpled self.

"I need to talk to you," Scott said. He looked nervous. "Can we talk in the hall?"

I followed him into the art gallery beside the lobby. Because it was summer, the white walls were empty except for scattered hooks and nails. Large, billowing, silver sculptures occupied the center of the room. I followed him behind one.

"Fuck it," he said dramatically and closed his eyes. He kissed me full on the mouth, bending over because he was so tall. As he squeezed my shoulders firmly, he continued to press his mouth against mine. I stared at him shocked, paralyzed, and deeply uncomfortable. Still, there was something undeniably appealing about being desired so much in one week. Who knew sexual connections were so readily available?

His thick tongue filled my mouth, gluing me in place. I tried to figure out how I felt about all this: his stubble against my skin, that he felt so much older, that he wasn't a woman. It didn't take long to realize I wasn't into it.

Scott's face was scrunched up in a blissed-out grimace. He breathed heavily into my mouth, pulling me closer. I automatically followed his movements, kissing back, wrapping my arm around him. I couldn't think of what else to do. I didn't want to ruin his moment or disappoint him. Then I heard the voices of people nearby and cringed. This was too much. I pushed Scott away.

"Okay," I said, attempting to sound friendly.

"I've wanted you so much."

I led him back to the lecture hall. "They'll be pissed if we miss the beginning."

The next night I told Maya about it while we lounged on my bed.

"Doesn't he know you're gay?"

"I don't know. I don't get it," I said, slightly relishing my new-found predicament.

She gripped my messy hair and tugged on the collar of my boy's polo shirt. "You look super gay," she said.

I was giddy when she nipped at my mouth and wrapped an arm around my waist, but in the middle of everything there was a knock on the door.

"You there?" It was Scott's deep voice.

Maya and I froze, wide-eyed, gripping each other. We stayed silent until he went away and then broke into giggles. I snorted into her neck, ashamed to be dissing Scott but thrilled to be in alliance with this cool girl.

We stayed in bed talking past curfew. Maya and I had never been in my room together so late at night and it felt different. I couldn't fully see her in the dark, and when we started kissing, it felt more deliberate and grown-up. Our whole bodies were touching. There was a lot of movement. Who's on top? Flipping. Sliding together. Our legs interlocked, and when my thigh pressed between her legs, she sighed. Then, by accident, I touched her breast. It hadn't occurred to me yet to do it on purpose.

"You want something?" she asked teasingly, glancing down at her chest.

I didn't know what to say. I'd barely considered the fact that she had breasts, let alone what I'd do if I could touch them, but Maya took her shirt off and so did I. Then we took our pants off and our underwear, and we were naked.

"I've never done this before," she whispered.

"Me either."

"Oh, come on," she said, rolling her eyes.

"No," I said seriously. "Not at all."

I tried stroking her stomach, thighs, nipples, hip, following the path of my hands with soft kisses. It was all lovely but it felt like nothing was really happening. Flustered, I pushed to get on my back. Maya boldly took a plunge and kissed her way down my body until she was on my clit, kissing and licking.

Jesus.

I gasped. My clit felt almost too sensitive like there was more sensation than I could bear. I rocked helplessly, lost in the feeling and aware of nothing but how amazing it felt.

When she stopped and sat up, Maya chuckled uncomfortably. "Easy, girl," she said.

Shame flooded my throat and my face grew hot. In the dark, I couldn't decipher her meaning. Was she angry at me? Had I been too loud? Was it not supposed to feel good? Why had she laughed? I'd let my guard down for a minute, and it seemed like something had gone wrong, but I couldn't figure out what.

Rattled, I moved to get back into a more familiar position. I kissed her neck and mouth, running my hands once again over her body. She leaned into me, apparently happy. She was so beautiful. She was smaller than me, which made some part of me feel unaccountably strong.

Maybe this is okay, I thought.

I really like her, I thought.

But, unlike a few minutes ago, I felt very separate. I felt like the pleasure I'd just experienced was alien and incomprehensible. Did Maya masturbate? Probably not—she was a girl; I was an anomaly. The stickiness between my legs felt excessive and inappropriate. I wished I could get rid of it. Did Maya really want to be here? Was I like Scott, intrusive and burdensome? My desire felt gross.

Maya was now flat on her back and her vulva looked very adult to me, even though we were the same age. Her pubic hair was different than mine, dark and thick and wild. I didn't know what to make of it, and I felt myself tumbling further into anxiety and isolation. I moved in a few times with my mouth, but I felt scared, unable to connect with this part of her body.

The room was dark and I felt alone. I felt like I did when I was a little kid and left overnight with an unsafe adult or when my mom screamed at me and chased me around the house. I stroked Maya's labia with my fingers, trying to do what I'd like on my body, trying to be one of the skillful queer women in all the erotica I'd read. But I was reaching my breaking point. There was this wonderful person in my bed who I was so into a few minutes ago but who now felt like a stranger, threatening and unreliable.

My desire for Maya had evoked a whole constellation of entwined memories and emotions, experiences from my past that I did not yet know how to make sense of. I didn't know then how to ask for the reassurance I needed. I couldn't ask *Do you want me the way I want you?*

"Is it okay if we take a break?" I asked, sounding more confident than I felt.

Maya agreed, and we curled up together.

Maya fell asleep, but I stayed awake, feeling lost and scared. Eventually I woke her up and asked if she'd go back to her room. I couldn't explain why I needed her to, and I felt guilty about kicking her out of my bed, especially when she looked so startled by my request.

The next morning I saw one of her earrings on my nightstand. It was sea green and dangly; my spirits rose as I held it. When I handed it to Maya in the cereal line at breakfast, it seemed like an outrageously adult transaction, passing this sexualized token between us. But as she put the earring in her pocket, I could tell she was hurt. When I tried to kiss her later, she ducked her head to avoid me.

I wish I'd known then about how sex involves all aspects of who we are, not just the sexy parts, and how, weirdly, that's a good thing. Talking about difficult feelings with a lover is the surest route I've found to incredible sex. There's nothing better than saying *I feel ashamed* and being met with the full reality of someone else's desire.

But that summer, talking with Maya about the sex between us didn't feel like an option. "I want . . . ," I'd begin, too embarrassed to tell her outright that I wanted to have sex.

We hung out a few more times but never regained that special connection. I remember the last night of the program. I watched Maya read in front of everyone. She was electric, slamming each and every word. All of us in the audience were silenced by the rocketing voice coming out of her.

So much of sex is about communication and what's remarkable is where that communication can take you. Sometimes I still wonder what would have happened if I had been able to talk with Maya— my lion poet.

In the previous story, Laurel struggled to find the words to tell Maya what she wanted and needed. It's not easy to talk about sex, especially when you're naked next to someone else. The words—vulva, cock, nipple, tongue—stick in our throats. We're not always sure what we have the right to ask for. We assume, perhaps, that bodies just know what to do when they get together.

In spite of all the movies, music, books, and magazines depicting and discussing sex, it's still overhyped and underexplained. Sex education curriculum in the United States is minimal and often downright terrifying. Parents struggle to talk with teens. The words don't come easy for them either. It's embarrassing and awkward and kind of weird.

This leaves many of us—like Sarah in the next story—to venture forth into the world of sex without a map.

8
Who Needs a Map?
Sarah Mirk

When I graduated from high school, all I wanted to do was get as far away as possible from everyone I knew. My parents were great but I had grown up in a small town in Southern California, the kind of place where you develop excellent skills at hiding from people in the grocery store. After years of being seen as the clean-cut smart kid I longed to kick everything familiar to the curb. I wanted to go to a place where I could make myself into whoever I wanted to be. When I told my parents I had been hired as a field organizer for some sort of "campaign to save the environment" in Portland, Oregon, and that I wanted to move up there for the three months between high school and college, I think they agreed to the plan mostly because I was supremely confident. I didn't know much but I felt good about myself and my body. I was a pretty fearless seventeen-year-old girl.

My mom helped me find a dorm room to rent for the summer on the city's west side. When I showed up to my first day of work, far from home, I quickly learned that "field organizer"

meant "canvasser" and "saving the environment" meant "fundraising." Each week, the organization brought in a crop of fourteen
new idealistic individuals—people who cared about the world
and desperately needed a paying job. There was a *Let's go, team!*
summer-camp feel to the office, with an undercurrent of the
uncomfortable reality that we needed to keep our spirits high
because fundraising is soul-crushing work.

We were given a few hours of training on current environmental
talking points and handed a clipboard with a hundred addresses. I
spent the long, hot days wandering around the suburbs of Portland
knocking on doors and asking strangers for money.

No one was happy to see me.

Ever.

I was immediately in awe of the veteran canvassers who ran the
office. Everyone who survived as a canvasser for more than a few
months was confident, tough, and absolutely gorgeous. Susanna
was a tanned, earthy ceramicist who wore a knife on her belt.
Josh had a lean swagger, a mop of hair, and John Lennon glasses.
Cheyenne was a tough, industrious hippie with short hair, a golden
smile, and the best laugh in the city. David had a movie-star jawline and a rough-cut face. Jeff had curly hair and seemed like the
kind of guy who excelled at Frisbee.

"Whose streets?!" they shouted. "Our streets!" we shouted
back.

If you missed your quota—eighty-six dollars—for two nights in
a row, it didn't matter how cool or peppy or experienced you were,
you would be automatically fired. Tension ran through the office
like a rubber band. We were a peppy, tight-knit crew always on the
verge of snapping.

I'm not sure if the humiliation of asking strangers for money was
worse than the rejection of being turned down ninety-five times
out of one hundred, but either way, I spent at least a few hours of
each shift sitting alone on the sidewalk. I would stare at the sky. I
would stare at the ground. I would stare at my hands. I would stare

at anything other than my list of doors and savor the few moments I had to myself.

After two weeks, I was the only person left from the group hired on my day. I was a professional, a survivor.

During those weeks, I discovered that you were supposed to be eighteen to work as a full-time canvasser. In the craziness of hiring and firing dozens of people a week, the office had forgotten to check my ID. Oops.

As we counted our money into piles at the end of the night, I responded to the older canvassers' questions about my life by spinning a fantasy identity, imagining where I'd be in a year when I really would be eighteen. I told them I had just finished my first year of college. I waxed on about my school's environmental group and about my dorm full of eccentric friends. I told great stories about the radio show I hosted on the campus station. I definitely wasn't a virgin—hell no! I divulged some choice details about my imaginary boyfriend. We'd had great sex but he'd been a jerk and I'd dumped him.

Each night after we'd wrapped up the financial paperwork, the veteran crowd would go out. They started to invite me out to bars and house parties. After a few weeks of working and partying together, we became real friends. Except that everything I told them was sort of a lie. I told myself that my identity wasn't so much a fabrication as not-yet-true but the fake stories kept a convenient wall between me and all the people who I thought were infinitely cooler than me.

I started to think about sex all the time. I'd walk into a house party full of twenty-three and twenty-four-year-olds (ancient!) and think about how I was the only virgin in the room.

I never liked the language around virginity. I hated the concept of *losing* part of myself, especially when it involved a guy *taking* it away. In high school, I'd seen a couple of close friends fall into relationships with guys whom they described as *sweet* and I described as *greasy*. These friends told me stories about going farther than they wanted to, about sweaty hands under their bras.

People built up virginity to be such a special, powerful thing, and I never wanted some man to have that much power over me. What if we shared some special thing and then he told his gross friends all about it? I felt like I could never trust a guy enough to give him my body.

But now I was very aware of being a virgin. The word ran through my head as I hung out on the edge of each house party. *Virgin, virgin, virgin.*

I didn't want to walk around with the word hanging around my neck as my friends downed cheap beer, but I was too nervous to get close enough to anyone to have sex either.

At those summer house parties I got good at snagging an empty Olympia can and filling it with water in the bathroom so I could sit there and sip along with everyone else. I felt like I needed to be in control of myself. Being sober made me feel safe. Each night, when it got late, the canvassers would start slurrily telling me how they had a lot of respect for me and I'd know it was time to leave.

I'd take the bus back downtown to my apartment. I was too proud to buy a map and I could never figure out where exactly my apartment was. I'd just wander around the streets, navigating by landmarks. With my headphones in, I followed the train tracks, took a left at the stadium, went up a hill. If I walked in a big enough circle, I'd eventually come across my own bendy road. My feet would hurt, and I'd flop on my dorm room bed, lights off, sheets off, alone.

I was afraid to even kiss anyone.

What else would they want?

After about six weeks, I was invited to join a "camping canvass." Many of the nonprofit's exploitive endeavors were branded as "fun opportunities," and I jumped at the chance to drive to Las Vegas, Nevada, with Jeff, David, and the usual crew. We pulled into Las Vegas just after dawn. I had accidentally left my wallet on my bed back in Portland so Jeff lent me $20, and I spent the next week

eating two meals a day at the Golden Nugget casino, which had a
$1.99 breakfast special.

The canvassing was the worst anyone had ever seen. The sub-
divisions were vast and hostile. I scraped by, barely making quota
every night until the last one, when a guy in another nondescript
tract home pulled a gun on me and told me to get off his lawn. I
spent the rest of my shift in an empty park, lying underneath the
swings and trying not to cry as I looked up at the big Nevada sky.

When we met up at the end of the night in a local brewery,
people who were over quota peeled donations off their piles and
handed them to me. Jeff, who was in charge, recorded them on my
tally. The week ended with all of us keeping our jobs. To celebrate,
everyone except for me got raging drunk

Jeff proposed a toast. "To being young and stupid!"

We all cheered.

The tediousness of the drive home was hysterical. We laughed
at road signs and played word games until we ran out of both
road signs and word games. In the desert near Mount Shasta, we
switched drivers, and I squeezed in back next to Jeff, our thighs and
arms touching through layers of sweat and cotton. He offered to
give me a neck massage. I turned sideways in my seat, and as he laid
his hands on my shoulders, the car seemed to disappear. He leaned
in and his breath raised the hair on my neck.

There was no horrible job. There was no guy in Las Vegas with
a gun. There was no eighty-six dollar quota. There was no week
of casino pancakes. I closed my eyes and there were just his hands
on my neck. He leaned his head against mine and I breathed in the
smell of him.

We stayed that way for what felt like three hundred miles.

At a party a few nights later, I got cornered by a raw foodist and
was enduring a lecture about dehydrators and numerology when I
caught Jeff's eye from across the room. He grabbed my hand and
led me upstairs. I don't know whose bedroom we locked ourselves
in but we made out on the filthy mattress until my lips hurt. We'd

gotten down to our underwear, and Jeff put his fingers up inside me. It was a surprise but it felt damn good. Drunk on lust, I got lost in sensations only to realize Jeff was whispering something to me.

"What?" I whispered back, hoarsely.

"Will you toss my cookies?" he murmured.

My body froze. I had no idea what *toss my cookies* meant. Was that even what he'd said? I didn't want to ask him to repeat himself or to let on that I had no idea what cookies were. Too proud for a map, I plunged onward, deciding the request must have something to do with touching his dick. I stuck my hand down his boxers and fumbled around. His penis felt like a bizarre, alien object, a fleshy Washington Monument. I was caught between horror and desperately trying to play it cool. I frantically fumbled around and managed to poke him hard in his swampy testicles. Then I rolled over and fell asleep. We woke up together, gross and groggy, and took the bus our separate ways.

Despite my clear ineptitude, the next night Jeff invited me out for a proper date: just us, no one else from work. We met up in Pioneer Square and talked about where we grew up and walked a few blocks to see his favorite fountain in the city. He was sweet. I felt good with him. He opened up to me about his life after college, his favorite people, his interests, and I felt bad that I wasn't being honest with him.

We meandered back from the cool downtown dusk to my dorm. The air in my little room was hot and stagnant. I didn't have any way to put on music—I'd been living in my headphones all summer—so we made out in silence on the narrow, plastic-sheeted bed. It was way too small for both of us so after some awkward snuggling, I grabbed the cushions off the suite's sofa, put them on the floor, and dragged my mattress down next to them. The lights were off, but we could still see each other in the light streaming through the small, locked window.

Now that we were here, in this moment, about to do exactly what I'd wanted to do, I got nervous. I didn't get self-conscious about my body, but I suddenly felt weird about his. I didn't know this person, I realized, with rising anxiety. His body was so foreign, so fuzzy, so lean. His chest and legs and arms felt strange and tough under my hands. His strange sweat was all over me. When he opened the condom wrapper, the unfamiliar, chemical smell hit me and I tensed. In this most intimate moment, I felt very alone.

But I was committed.

This was the way to escape virginity, to destroy its power over me. I had to go it alone.

I lay still underneath him as his penis pushed inside me. I both wanted him there and didn't want him there at all. I tried to keep my hands on him while my brain floated away. I kept my eyes squeezed shut and thought about how soon it would be over. I wasn't paying attention to his thrusting or the way that it felt both a little painful and a little good, I distracted myself by thinking in intense detail about what we'd do the next day. Would we get coffee after? How would we walk there? Should I try to make breakfast? What groceries did I have? Was the milk in the fridge expired? Maybe it was expired. Very quickly, it seemed like his body shivered and he stopped. I came back to reality. He slid out of me and leaned up to my face, kissing me. He felt cold with sweat and I still didn't open my eyes. The whole thing felt absurd, like something animals did, not even a part of me or who I was.

I was grateful to fall asleep and wake up a few hours later as myself, having gone through this undesirable ritual. We rose early and walked to the coffee shop like I'd seen in my head. We made pleasant small talk as I walked Jeff to his bus stop and kissed him good-bye. My flight back home was the next day and I never saw him again.

• • • • • •

That year at college, I did help out at the radio station. I did join the environmental club. I did make friends with the adventurous,

eccentric girls on my hall. And I met a boy who became my best
friend and then my boyfriend. Before we had sex, we talked about
our histories. It felt *good* being honest with him. We confessed the
things we were nervous to do and laughed about the things we
liked.

Slowly, I let my anxious boundaries dissolve and was surprised
to find that trusting someone made me stronger not weaker. Just
as I'd imagined for my future self, we had lots of sex. But he didn't
wield desire over my head like a weapon or abandon me when I
revealed myself. Back in high school, I could never have imagined
this sweet spot—a friend with whom I could safely shed my armor,
someone I could learn from, and whom I would want to have stick
around and know me for years. Being young and stupid is fun, but
being young and honest is even better.

Many women feel their relationship to their own bodies is a stumbling block to good sexual experiences. In the pursuit of some imaginary ideal, you might be pretty hard on yourself: Look at my bulging tummy, teeny breasts, bushy pubes, lumpy thighs, enormous cleavage, scrawny ass. I hate my zitty skin, sweaty armpits, bony knees. My period.

It's exhausting to worry so much about how you look and smell and feel.

But maybe you don't have to agonize. Maybe none of it matters. Maybe when you're with someone who really loves you, every single inch of you will be good.

So good.

{ We swam in a pool of sex, or at least the idea of having sex, and the water was fine. }

{ . . . in the back seats of cars and in the hayloft and once, sticky with the juice of a stolen watermelon spiked with vodka, in the middle of an abandoned blacktop road. }

{ We took off the rest of our clothes in about five seconds. }

9

Power in the Blood

Molly Bloom

It happened in that singular summer: those sultry months that separate high school from college. We swam in a pool of sex, or at least the idea of having sex, and the water was fine. DJs hired for our high school dances in this rural Midwestern town were known to introduce slow songs by saying, "Ladies, here's your chance to polish your man's belt buckle."

Yes, they did say that.

I was eighteen, and by that time I had brought a few of those large, elaborately decorated cowboy belt buckles to a high shine. Of course, I brought a high shine to my own damn self during those slow dances—and after, in the back seats of cars and in the hayloft and once, sticky with the juice of a stolen watermelon spiked with vodka, in the middle of an abandoned blacktop road.

I was raised in a conservative Baptist home where there was no discussion about safe sex or any kind of sex for that matter. No sex before marriage was a given. I considered myself a virgin, although I suspected that I possessed that title only on a technicality. I'd done everything up to actual penetration, and until Sam came along I was okay with that. It allowed me to think of myself as a "good girl."

Things were different that summer. I'd been dating Sam for nine months. He was a year behind me in school and, while we both cared deeply for each other, we knew that our relationship might very well end when I went to college in the fall. So it took on a fierce intimacy, as if we could somehow forestall the changes to come.

We always stopped just short of making love, frustrating as it was. We may have been young but we weren't foolish. We weren't taking any chances on an unintended pregnancy—not an unusual occurrence in our small town—but getting birth control was a dicey prospect. We knew the owner of the drugstore and he knew our parents. You couldn't just waltz in and buy a package of condoms.

One night, we were doing a lot of enthusiastic fooling around behind the barn. We were both highly aroused and one of us said, for probably the millionth time, "I wish we could do it."

And then it occurred to me—maybe we could. I was on the second day of my period, and I thought this was probably the one totally safe time of the month to have sex. (I was wrong, of course. It's rare, but women can in fact become pregnant during menstruation.)

I was game, but what if Sam was totally turned off by the idea? My body told my brain to stop worrying and go for it.

"Um, I'm having my period now," I whispered.

"That's okay," he said, his mouth on my nipple. "I don't mind."

"I mean, it's a safe time for us to do it. If it doesn't gross you out." I waited for any sign of disgust.

Sam didn't hesitate. "Gross me out? Hell no!"

"It might be kind of messy," I said. "You'll get all bloody."

He grinned. "I don't mind. I've been bloody before."

"Not there, I bet," I teased.

We took off the rest of our clothes in about five seconds. The sight of Sam's slim, athletic nakedness made me gasp. I removed my tampon and threw it into the bushes. I wondered briefly if some wild animal would bring that deliciously bloody thing back to its den. Better than Sam's father finding it the next day.

Between my arousal and the blood, I was plenty wet, and he entered me easily. The sex was great—amazing—blood and all. Afterward, we cleaned up with some tissues I found in my purse, giggling in sudden self-conscious embarrassment at what we'd just done. We'd lost our virginities in a sea of menstrual blood.

I drove home that night thinking about what a great guy Sam was. I was pretty sure that most guys would have recoiled at the very thought of having sex with a girl who was having her period. It probably helped that both of us lived on farms. We saw and experienced life in all of its beautiful and ugly messiness, from birth to death. Hell, what's a little blood? And who am I kidding? It probably helped that we were two horny teenagers.

Even so, menstruation was seen as dirty and shameful. We lived in monthly dread that a tampon would fall out of our lockers, or that we'd bleed through onto our stonewashed blue jeans. Remember that scene in Stephen King's *Carrie*, in which the main character gets her first period in the locker room? Her crazy mother hasn't given her a heads-up and Carrie naturally thinks she is dying. And how do the other girls react? They throw tampons and sanitary napkins at her. It's the ultimate public humiliation, reinforced by the pig's blood at the prom.

Menstrual etiquette dictated that, while you might complain about *that time of the month* to your girlfriends, it was otherwise a closely held secret. Ridiculous tampon commercials assured us that if we used their products we'd spend our periods in delirious happiness, frolicking on the beach in white bikinis and going horseback riding. No one would know about our "little secret."

This idea that menstrual blood is somehow dirty isn't new, of course; it's part of our cultural DNA. Menstruating women were, and often still are, considered unclean in many religious traditions. Contact with a menstruating woman—not to mention sex!—was bad juju.

I'm no longer a Baptist or very religious in any way but I can't help but think of the old Baptist hymn *There Is Power in the Blood*. It begins, "Would you be free from the burden of sin? There's pow'r in the blood, pow'r in the blood." Although the hymn refers to the blood that the crucified Jesus shed for our sins, it makes me think of the power of my own blood. It gave me the power to make my own choice about sex that night. My blood made me free from the burden, not of sin, but of worry. Sam and I managed to score some condoms that summer, and it was a good thing too. Having made love once, I'm pretty sure we wouldn't have had the self-control to stop doing it.

I went off to college that fall and, predictably, we broke up soon after the homecoming dance. We were going different places: Sam wanted to be a farmer and I dreamed of the big city. But I still give him a lot of credit for his enthusiastic embrace of me and my body—especially at that time of the month.

Thank you, Sam.

Pink, blue. Girl, boy. Gay, straight. Virgin, not.

It's tempting to line up the little boxes and get everyone to jump into one. But forget the tidy categories. Reality can be much more complicated, especially when it comes to sexual attraction. Why does that woman with the dreadlocks make my heart race? Why do I flush every time I see that guy with the fish tattoo?

Arousal is unpredictable. Sometimes it grows slowly out of a deep emotional connection. Sometimes it bursts out of nowhere, a powerful physical reaction that surprises us with its ferocity.

Just as we go through phases where we feel more or less sexual, we can also experience fluid patterns of attraction that change throughout our lives. In the next story, Sara shares how a growing understanding of her sexual identity influences how she views the world and her place in it.

> Even when we were able to proceed without **interruptions**, things didn't go smoothly . . . .

> Her hands unhooking hooks . . . The scent of her hair. Her **breath** on the back of my neck. The moment right before we kissed.

> Being a girl who **wanted** a girlfriend was not so simple.

10
"Openly Bisexual"
Sara Ryan

The last time I had to explain about my sexual identity,[1] I was in a speeding car along I-35 on an unseasonably cold day in Texas. Okay, I didn't *have* to, per se. But the friend who was driving was curious. We'd met through the young adult author community, so he knew my work and he knew that I identified as queer. But I'd, in quick succession, mentioned a workshop for emerging LGBTQ voices I was excited to be teaching and then said something about my husband. And although he didn't come right out (as it were) and ask, I had the impression that the juxtaposition of these two pieces of information was somehow surprising.

So I told him the latest version of what I say when people want to know how it works for me. Yes, I've had significant relationships with people of different genders (and by that I mean both with

---

1 As of this writing. By the time this book is published, it's entirely possible that I will have had several more versions of the conversation.

cis[2] men and cis women, and with people whose sense of gender is more fluid and shifting). No, it doesn't mean I'm automatically looking to hook up with everybody all the time. No, it's not a phase. No, I'm not experimenting.

"I think of it as a lens that informs how I understand and navigate the world," I said finally.

"Maybe this is off base, but it kind of reminds me of being biracial," he said. "Like, you don't feel like you really fit in on either side."

I'd have been hesitant to make that analogy myself because I can't know how being biracial feels. But I appreciated his willingness to use an aspect of his own identity as a way to better understand mine.

Let me assure you that I did not always have the ability to explain my sexual identity to others, or even to myself. I had to analyze, interrogate, worry,[3] discuss, research—and write about it in journals.

I called the journal I kept when I was fifteen *L.B.B.*, short for Little Black Book. I think I knew that the phrase *little black book* was typically used to describe a collection of women's phone numbers kept by a man, but since the journal literally was a little black book, it seemed appropriate.

1.

My second summer in the theater group, the summer I was fifteen, Ursula knew I was going to have sex with Robert before I did. Ursula was older, in her twenties: funny, mechanically adept, a martial artist into puns, comics, gaming, science fiction, and fantasy. She knew a lot of things I didn't but she was never

---

2 Via Wikipedia: Cisgender and cissexual (often abbreviated to simply cis) describe related types of gender identity where individuals' experiences of their own gender match the sex they were assigned at birth.

3 Both in the sense of "fret" and in the sense of "drag around with the teeth, as of a dog or other carnivorous animal."

condescending and always treated me as a friend and a peer. She'd
observed Robert and me as we were getting together. The joke
was that we were "the lame leading the blind," since I was on
crutches that summer and he was, in fact, blind. Before him, I'd
barely even been on any dates. Though I'd had multiple crushes,
not all of which I initially recognized as such, despite my tendency
to analyze everything in my life in minute detail (usually, as stated
above, in my journal).

We moved fast. After two dates, we had this conversation, which
I recorded in L.B.B:

Dear L.B.B.—

Robert asked me what I was afraid of. I said:
"Is this an all-embracing question or—"
"Context, dear, context."
"I thought so—I don't know—going too fast, I suppose—all
the classic things one is supposed to be afraid of."[4]

Now I see that what I am really afraid of is the next logical
step in this process[5]—or at least I am at this point. I want
to stay where we are now for a while at least. Of course,
looming off in the distance is the perennial concern[6] which
I'm not even going to think about until this has lasted much
longer than it has and "things" have gone much further.
Robert says "I'm not in this for a 'quick one'—I do care about
you and *I am patient.*" Homemade italics are mine.

Two entries after that one:

---

4   Yes, we actually talked like this.

5   By that I think I meant touching below the waist.

6   Sex. Or maybe birth control?

Dear L.B.B.—

I do love Robert and I decided that if I was protected, I would make love[7] with him. But I want a second opinion, really. Help me, L.B.B: what's a convenient and conversational way to say "Excuse me, Reverend, but is premarital sex a sin in God's eyes? And as long as we're on the subject, how about in yours?"

And the next one after that:

Dear L.B.B.—

The more I consider it, the more certain I become: I want to share all[8] with Robert. Does this make me immoral? Define morality. I am biologically, mentally, and emotionally mature. Age is irrelevant. Sex is not sin. And this is anything but a sin. I love Robert and he loves me. We are both responsible. I can see no danger. Certainly I am nervous, but eager. And I know he is. I will not be a tease saying, "This much and no more." There is no reason to be. I dislike the fact that I must be practical—I don't like the idea of "coupling without touching"[9]—but that is the way that it must be if it is to be.

I don't think my reasons are the classic teenage ones—I'll list those I think of offhand and shoot them down.

- Everybody's doing it. I don't know if they are, I don't have the data, and in any case it is irrelevant.

---

7   As an adult I am not a fan of the phrase "make love"; it seems cheesy. At the time, I thought it conveyed the deeply meaningful nature of the activity.

8   Again with the cheesy.

9   I think I got this engineering-tinged phrase from a late Robert A. Heinlein novel—which, by the way, I do not recommend as a source for understanding interpersonal relationships—but I can't swear to it. What I meant was using a condom.

- I'll lose him if I don't. No. The conviction I have against that is so deep I won't even dignify it with further answer. That is a main reason in my decision to anyway.

I have found out an interesting thing: not only, when it happens, will it be my first time, and collectively our first time, it will also be his first time. This surprised me somewhat. Don't laugh (hypothetical future reader to whom I am speaking)[10] but I'm thinking seriously about finding a copy of the Kama Sutra or other similar work and studying it.

It was about this time that Ursula invited me to dinner. Ursula had her own apartment and a commitment to sharing useful information with younger friends. I don't remember what we ate but I remember what we talked about: birth control, in more detail than my health classes had ever covered, with a copy of *Our Bodies, Ourselves*[11] accompanied by her commentary on the pros and cons of various methods.[12] We didn't talk at all about sex itself; the entire focus was on what to expect if I didn't want to be expecting.[13]

We'd had previous discussions about sexuality; she was bisexual, she'd told me, and I filed the information away. The term illuminated possibilities, although I didn't immediately connect it with, for instance, the girl in my junior high choir whose solos and dark eyes I'd found equally riveting. I was a shy and frequently embarrassed person, and as such it was sometimes difficult for me to pinpoint the reason why I might at any given time be blushing.

---

10 Yes, I really did address future readers in my teenage diaries. I apologize.

11 Feminist health guide focused on helping women understand and have agency over their own bodies. Already a classic by the time I encountered it.

12 Why wasn't Robert invited too? Maybe because, despite Ursula's overall progressive views, birth control still seemed like something that I, as the person in the relationship who could get pregnant, should handle.

13 *What To Expect When You're Expecting* being a standard reference book about pregnancy.

Besides, that junior high choir soloist was more popular than I was;
if I allowed myself to think at all about why her lovely voice and
face made me flush and shiver, no doubt I concluded it was due to
a desire to be more like her, rather than more near her.

After that dinner with Ursula, my nervous, giddy anticipation of
the impending event with Robert coexisted with a sense of responsibility. I was embarking on something serious, something that
required equipment. Also, I was preoccupied with my weight and
apt to be overtaken by paralyzing self-consciousness. What, aside
from my desire for Robert and my confidence in his for me, made
me able to seriously consider being sexually intimate so quickly?

I never wrote about this then, but I think his blindness helped.
Of course, I knew intellectually that he'd learn the contours of my
body via touch, and, less intellectually, I knew that I wanted him
to—but there was also something comforting about knowing that
whatever we were doing, he wouldn't be able to see me.

My paralyzing self-consciousness meant that even though I was
able to make a mature decision about the need to acquire birth
control, I initially didn't go to a pharmacy. I went to a gift and
novelty shop.

Dear L.B.B.—

I made a purchase today. One of the items will be a hostess
gift for Marie who is, in theory, having a "hellacious bash"
when her parents go out of town later this month. The
other is for personal use. They are identical. Okay, slavering
scandal-seekers, this is the product: "Condomints™, Sex
that's truly tasteful! Practice safe sex *and* fresh breath—Now
that's sex in good taste! The product that says 'Don't give me
something to remember you by.'* *In our opinion, truly safe sex
can only be achieved by locking yourself in a room with yourself."*
This resembles a large matchbook; when opened, contains a
package of two breath mints and a prophylactic.

While I was acquiring Condomints, Robert was working on another necessary element in the sex equation: securing a time when the tiny bedroom he shared—he, fortunately I think in retrospect, had the bottom bunk—would be vacant. Robert, like Ursula, had an apartment—a basement apartment close to campus—but he had two roommates, both of whom were, while mostly amused by and approving of his rapidly developing relationship with me, also not always inclined to disrupt their own schedules to grant us privacy.

Then I steeled myself to get hold of another form of birth control to supplement the novelty condom. Ursula had told me that it was better to have multiple methods of protection, and in case this isn't already clear from the journal entries, I was, while gung-ho, very cautious.

Dear L.B.B.—

I am extremely proud of myself. I walked to the pharmacy.
I looked at the foam.[14] I read the label. I took the container
out of the package.[15] I said, "Oh, shit," and walked out of the
pharmacy. Down the street. To the traffic light. Then I said to
myself, "Sara, snap out of this. It's worthless," turned around,
marched determinedly back to the pharmacy, picked up the
foam and bought it.

Thus, we were prepared.
Preparation, however, did not ensure that the consummation we devoutly wished for would occur without difficulty. We were interrupted by one or another of his roommates multiple times,

---

14 Spermicidal foam, that is. It came with a handy applicator, which you'd think would mean it'd be easy to use.

15 Just to contemplate it, I hasten to add, not to stash it away and shoplift it. But I neglected to write in my journal that I put it back in the package before leaving the store, and I'm giving you the unaltered record.

one of the hazards of undertaking intimacy in a tiny shared apartment. (Another hazard: the bedroom's decor included a Bruce Lee
poster that sometimes seemed to be staring with disapproval at our
endeavors.) Even when we were able to proceed without interrup-
tions, things didn't go smoothly:

Dear L.B.B.—

"How to Get Fucked while Remaining a Virgin!"
In our last episode, as you no doubt recall, well, anyway—
Our story opens in Corsica, where out on the veranda is a
bearded man in glasses, conducting a small choir[16]—Sorry.
No. Wrong. Let us start in fact at the beginning. Well,
after more debate, a lot in fact, I went once more to foam
myself and got foam all over myself. Hysterics began there.
Then we once more made the attempt and the goddamned
thing[17] still wouldn't fucking stay on (or wouldn't stay on for
fucking). This was very frustrating but still hilarious.

Eventually we managed. Although I shockingly failed to doc-
ument this, I'm pretty sure I remember that after we'd struggled
passionately for a while to position ourselves in an optimal fashion
he asked if I knew the definition of a nice girl, and when I didn't,
he explained that a nice girl puts it in for you, and we laughed some
more and then I did.

Dear L.B.B.—

My God, I can't believe it, it finally happened. It was beyond
description and I did not want to move, but we had to, to

---

16   For some reason I am quoting here from the Beatles, "Everywhere It's Christmas."

17   The condom, aka.

take off the condom. Well, I'll go on the pill ASAP and then we won't need to worry about that.[18]

. . .

I'm a mutant or something 'cause it didn't hurt the first time. No virgin's blood either—I don't know, perhaps it's a myth perpetuated by the opposition.

2.

Between ages fifteen and nineteen, I determined that "bisexual" was a reasonable description of my sexuality. (I was uninformed at that point about the limitations of the gender binary.[19]) I recognized my crushes on girls as such. I sought out books and comics and movies that featured relationships between women. (They weren't easy to find.) My journal was a larger version of the same black notebook, and so, inevitably, I called it Big Black Book, abbreviated B^3. Some entries from the summer before I started college:

B^3—

Now I am reading *The Diary of Anaïs Nin*, the first two volumes. She certainly has a more literary style in her diary than I do here. But that is okay. I came to the conclusion that I haven't quite lived enough to write a lot of things. [...] Nin's writing has made me consider my bisexuality in a new light. She defines lesbianism as self-love. But I cannot agree with any theory that presupposes gender-specific characteristics. I don't think that man is this and woman is that and that one

---

18   This is followed by a marginal comment: "No, I won't. It's not safe and I'm too forget-ful." I'd learned from Ursula that it was extremely important to take the pill every day and I wasn't sure I could manage that. Plus, there was a lot of fear about poten-tial side effects. So I didn't go on the pill; we kept using both condoms and foam.

19   Definition via the Geek Feminism Wiki: " . . . the artificial division of the world into things that are 'masculine' or 'for men' and things that are 'feminine' or 'for women.' One of the starkest ways to think of this is to consider the phrase 'opposite sexes/ genders' (as opposed to 'different sexes/genders')."

can describe sexual traits. That in fact explains my own idea:[20]
I am not attracted to a sex;[21] I am attracted to people.

B^3—

How could I just blithely say "I'm bisexual?" That was
very easy for me. Didn't have to come out to my parents[22]
didn't have to get into the lifestyle,[23] just thought, okay, I'm
attracted to women, how about that?
This minidiatribe springs from reading *Rubyfruit Jungle*.[24]
Am I promiscuous??[25]
I'm not just saying I'm bi to be politically correct, I have
ached, sometimes, looking at women.
Why am I so fucked up? How can a book get to me this
much?

Deciding to have sex with Robert had involved some debate with
myself—*Was I the kind of girl who had premarital sex?*—but deciding to *date* him had been nothing but thrilling; a smart, funny,
attractive person was into me! Cultural reinforcement about the
swellness of being a girl with a boyfriend was all around.
    Being a girl who wanted a girlfriend was not so simple.
    When I made my first lesbian friends—a couple—they smiled
and nodded at my tentative attempts to assert nonheterosexual

---

20   It was certainly not just "my own idea," but it was a new idea for me.

21   Sex and gender are not synonymous, but I didn't know that yet.

22   I did, eventually, and they were supportive.

23   At the time, "the gay lifestyle" was a frequently used derogatory phrase, not unlike
     "the gay agenda." I'm not sure what all exactly I imagined it to encompass.

24   A lesbian coming-of-age novel first published in 1973 by Rita Mae Brown.

25   It was hard for me not to conclude that feeling any sexual desire at all meant that
     I was a slut. Admitting to myself that my desire was not restricted to one gender
     seemed to mean I was especially, worrisomely excessive and out of control.

status. They tried to set me up with one of their friends, a gorgeous, self-effacing grad student. We smiled and nodded at each other but nothing happened.

By then, sometimes I even said out loud that I was bisexual. ("You're a dyke," my lesbian friends said, comfortingly.) But I also felt that until I had sex with a woman, it would be somehow dishonorable or dishonest to really claim the sexual identity that seemed to best describe my patterns of attraction.[26] Sure, I'd look at women, sometimes strangers, sometimes, more confusingly, friends, and find myself overcome (and aching, as that overwrought journal entry states) about the things I was imagining us doing. Women with short hair and short nails, strong arms and unshaved legs, leather jackets and swagger; women with filmy scarves, intriguing perfumes, silk skirts, multiple bracelets; women who mixed it up: dresses and combat boots, T-shirts and crinolines.

But until I was in her arms, or hers, or hers, how could I say all that desire really counted?

I started wearing "freedom rings"[27] on a ball chain necklace to publicly signify my queerness. T-shirts proclaiming *Nobody Knows I'm a Lesbian* were popular with the proud dykes in my college town. When I spotted my first *Nobody Believes I'm Bisexual* shirt, I laughed out loud but was too shy to buy one of my own. I did, eventually, buy a shirt emblazoned with bisexual pride slogans as a tiny consumer act of identity-claiming—but then I was too shy to wear it, since many of the slogans seemed to me to overly emphasize the *sex* in bisexual.[28]

---

26 Again, I was underinformed about the complex nature of gender identity; one of the issues I now have with the word "bisexual" is that it suggests that there are (a) only two sexes, and (b) that sex and gender are synonymous.

27 A set of six anodized aluminum rings: one each in red, orange, yellow, green, blue, and purple, designed by David Spada in 1991. Freedom rings were described by Lindsy Van Gelder in the *New York Times* as "a way for gay people to flaunt their wholesomeness." But to me, it felt transgressive and a little dangerous to put them on.

28 I can't remember all of them—the shirt was dense with text—but I recall "How long can I stay in this phase?" "I'm a Kinsey Pi," and "Political lesbianism—not my idea of fun on a Saturday night."

I was so shy, in fact, that my second first time might not have happened without *The Rocky Horror Picture Show.* I'd been painfully attracted to Remedios since we'd met. Some of the attraction was mental—she knew so much that I wanted to know, about surrealism and literature and fashion and music and bigger cities than I'd ever lived in or even visited—but I was also desperate to touch her.

She said, "You were born to be Columbia."

She was an expert; she'd played another of the *Rocky* characters, Magenta, and would be dressing up accordingly when we went to the show with other friends.

Looking back at my journals, I see that I'd first heard about *Rocky* way back when I was fourteen, my first year with the theater group, because I wrote about the possibility of inviting my new friends to *Rocky Horror* for my birthday. (I didn't, in part because my curfew and the midnight showtime were simultaneous.) But all I knew about the film before Remedios told me how crucial it was included: (a) you were supposed to dress up somehow, it was (b) sexy, (c) scary, and (d) in addition to dressing up, you had to participate in other ways that remained obscure. If I'd had more information, I might have been given hope by the fact that, in the film, Columbia and Magenta make out.

Remedios explained that in order to experience *Rocky Horror* correctly, I needed to dress appropriately, which in this context meant conforming to a sexy Goth aesthetic very unlike my usual look of T-shirts and jeans. It would be fine, though, since Remedios had garments I could borrow: fishnet stockings, a bustier, and a semi-transparent black lace skirt. Another friend provided high-heeled boots, and I made myself up with theatrical whiteface and baby powder and a lot of black eyebrow pencil and bright, bright red lipstick. The outfit was tricky to get into, featuring many intricate fastenings located in difficult-to-reach places. But it was a costume. I understood about costumes. You put them on to perform.

I watched the film; I watched Remedios. I followed her and my other friends' prompting about the audience participation, shocked and thrilled to sing the alternative lyrics to *There's A Light (Over At The Frankenstein Place)*: "There's a dyke . . . over at the Frankenstein place/There's a dy-i-i-i-i-ike/Sitting on her girlfriend's fa-ace/There's a dy-i-ike, a DY-ike, in the closet of eh-eh-vree-hee-body's wife."

I wasn't totally clear on why sitting on a girlfriend's face would be pleasurable for either party, but just loudly singing the word *dyke* multiple times in some version of public made me feel triumphant.

My ensemble was not very comfortable, especially after a couple hours' worth of enthusiastic audience participation, including a kick line that did the fishnets no favors. But I was grateful for it and all its fastenings because when we got back from the movie, it gave me the excuse to ask Remedios: "Um, could you help me take my clothes off?"

Both of us, I think, pretended I was asking purely because I didn't want to inadvertently damage the outfit's components.

The room was so small, and that made it easier: the bed was right there. Her hands unhooking hooks. Me hoping against hope that the ploy I couldn't even quite admit to myself was a ploy would work. The scent of her hair. Her breath on the back of my neck. The moment right before we kissed.

I wish that I'd written as much in my journal about us as I did about me and Robert, but by the time Remedios helped me take my clothes off I was writing fewer journal entries and more fiction.

I don't think either of us knew exactly what we were doing but we were enthusiastic about figuring it out. I'd read *Dykes to Watch Out For.*[29] She'd seen *Liquid Sky.*[30] We extrapolated, an exercise in juxtapositions. *Hands here? Lips there? Breasts! How do we arrange our legs to enable maximum friction?* I felt like I was getting away with

---

29 The genius comic that Alison Bechdel did for many years before she got broader recognition for her graphic memoir *Fun Home.*

30 I still haven't seen it; it's a cult film with aliens that feed on the pheromones released through heroin usage and also orgasms. Much dramatic New Wave fashion is involved, and apparently at least one instructive lesbian sex scene.

something, giggly and smug. When we curled together, finally, to sleep, I was content, exhausted, and *relieved* that we'd arrived at delightful solutions to the clichéd mystery: what do women do together?

I will also admit that I felt I'd become *real* as a queer person.

And I lasted, if I recall correctly, one whole entire day before I started worrying about what it meant, what we meant to each other, and whether it would happen again.[31]

. . . .

Okay, I imagine you asking, *but was the sex, you know, hotter with him or with her?*

It was *different*, and the ways in which it was different are not reducible to differences in anatomy. Every time I've acted on an attraction, I've had a constellation of reasons, from a person's scent and strength and stance to the kind of heady thrill that comes from feeling simultaneously understood, appreciated, and challenged.

Sometimes people ask, "Why do you still call yourself queer?" As though my queer passport has expired. As though my husband erases my history.

Honestly, it makes me tired.

But it also makes me aware, over and over again, of the importance of remaining visible. I don't know who created my Wikipedia entry, but despite my preference for the word *queer* as a descriptor,[32] I'm glad it includes the phrase *openly bisexual.* I no longer feel an insistent need to prove my sexual identity, but it doesn't hurt to have a reference source to cite.

---

31 It did, but our relationship rapidly became fraught and complicated, which was pretty much the theme of my romantic and sexual life through most of my twenties.

32 It feels both inclusive and concise.

Over and over in these essays we see women striving to understand themselves, to explore their sexual selves, and to find their own truth. Up until now, we've heard from women who do not question their womanness.

But just as sexual orientation can be fluid, so can gender.

Gender identity goes beyond the physical. It's the way we perceive ourselves on a spectrum from maleness to femaleness.

When gender—the truth of how we view ourselves—does not map to physical traits, the task of coming into our own as sexual beings can be much more challenging, as you'll see in Alex's story.

11

Iterum Vivere, to Live Anew

Alex Meeks

I lost my virginity eight years *after* the first time I had consensual intercourse.

I know this flies in the face of everything we learn about the meaning of virginity. It's not supposed to be a lizard's tail, regenerating once it's gone. But the real world doesn't always fit into neatly defined boxes. Our lives and experiences don't always follow the rules.

I grew up in Appalachia in a double-wide trailer in the woods surrounded by farmland. My childhood was, for the most part, unremarkable. My father worked long hours doing hard physical labor. My mother was a part-time beautician and full-time mother of three. My brothers and I spent the days exploring our vast deciduous playground. I would come inside after a long day of hard play, bruised and scraped and dirty. Looking back, I suppose I could call myself a tomboy. But in those days I was just a little boy, no "tom" needed.

I knew from an early age that I was somehow different from all the other little boys. I liked my hair long. I colored my fingernails with markers, which the teacher always made me wash off. I played the flute, loved to bake and sew, and preferred cats over dogs— things that shouldn't be gendered but are in small towns across America. My nightly prayers always included a plea to God that I would wake up a girl.

I rarely had any interest in school yard romance. When I did it was because I thought I was supposed to, not because I really wanted to. As my classmates and I grew older, shows of romantic longing seemed to become compulsory. And as high school approached it became very clear that if I didn't show interest in finding a girl-friend, something was wrong with me. I knew I wasn't like my peers but I tried my best to keep them from seeing that. I found a date to my eighth grade promotion dance, held in our school cafe-teria. I played the part. I gave my date a wrist corsage, walked into the dance with linked arms, slow-danced to the best country music of the late 1990s. I kept my hands well above my date's hips and danced just close enough to her not to arouse any suspicion that I didn't really want to be there. But it felt all wrong.

Then came high school. Suddenly most of the other boys were participating in a race to have sex. I found a girlfriend and convinced myself that I loved her. We spent long hours on the marching band bus holding hands, cuddling close. Eventually that led to making out on the dark trips home, hiding our heads from the chaperones as best we could. We progressed to awkward groping, exploring each other's bodies under the cover of a Marching Warriors blan-ket. Our relationship lasted the length of my sophomore marching band season before we broke up. She claimed that she wasn't ready to have a boyfriend and that we were moving too fast. I pretended to be heartbroken but in reality felt relief.

Our breakup lasted until the next fall. After a long trip home from a football game, we decided that it was time to finally take the plunge. We parked behind an isolated church, got into the backseat, and immediately we fell into each other. We ripped off our clothes, kissed each other deeply, and before I could process what was really happening, we were each having our very first penetrative sex. It was sweaty and awkward. Kenny Chesney was crooning on the radio. It felt fantastic in the tactile sense but I was emotionally detached from the experience. After we finished, we got dressed, and she drove me home in complete silence. She transferred to another school a couple of months later, and we never spoke again.

Everyone at my school seemed to suspect that I was queer. Even after word broke that I'd actually had heterosexual sex, people knew I wasn't straight. I got teased and bullied by the other kids, mostly by the athletic and popular types. One boy in particular—a pudgy, acne-riddled member of one of the less successful sports teams—was relentless. I did my best to avoid interacting with him, yet somehow my very existence was enough for him to seek me out. If I was going to be queer, then he wouldn't let me be happy.

But then, one spring evening as I was leaving a late jazz band practice, he approached me in the boys' room. As he slowly moved close to me with balled fists, I thought I was about to get the beating of a lifetime. I started shaking, and just as I started to cry, he kissed me. It wasn't a romantic kiss. It was barely even a lustful kiss. But finally, after years of simultaneous denial and hope for a moment like this, it was happening.

Neither of us spoke a word as we went into the farthest stall from the door. With only spit and the lubricant from his condom fighting the friction, he thrust himself into me. The pain was immediate and intense. I didn't think sex was supposed to feel like this but I had limited knowledge of the mechanics of anal sex. Maybe it was supposed to hurt the first time. I'd always heard that was true for a girl's first time being penetrated so why would it be different for me? I found it difficult to stay quiet enough not to get caught but that proved irrelevant because it was over almost as quickly as it began.

For the second time, I thought I had really lost my virginity.

For the second time, I feigned joy, all the while feeling detached.

Over the next several years, I had sexual encounters with a number of folks, both male and female. Accepting my queerness made my sex life better but something still felt wrong. I went away to college, and on a small liberal arts campus far from home, I found the language to understand what was so different about me. I learned that transgender people really do exist, and not just as drag queens or fetishistic transvestites paraded on the trashy daytime television shows. In this brand-new world, I learned that even though my birth certificate says *male*, I didn't have to be someone I'm not.

I came out as trans during my first semester on campus. As my understanding of myself grew and my identity evolved, I found myself in a community that embraced me for who I was. When my friends' parents would meet me and later ask whether I was a man or a woman, my friends often replied *Does it really matter?* or *That's Alex Meeks.*

But while my social circle began to recognize me as feminine or transcending gender, some things still weren't right. I felt like partners were having sex with me as they would with a man and I was not bringing my true identity into the bedroom. I only knew how to have sex *like a man*. I didn't know how to view my genitalia as anything other than masculine. Even when I slept with chasers, people who fetishize trans bodies and experiences, I still felt that I was being viewed sexually as a man. I felt doomed to eternal disconnection from my body, emotionally absent as I experienced physical intimacy and pleasure.

But then, two years after I graduated from college, I met Drew. My roommate and a friend visiting from out of town were at a dive bar in the small town where I lived, and they invited me to join them. We were enjoying cheap beer and stimulating conversation when this beautiful man walked right over to our table and sat down across from me. Until my roommate introduced us, I hadn't realized our friend had brought a roommate along for the trip. Drew was the kind of attractive that made it hard for me to speak. We talked about the mundane sorts of things people discuss while hanging out at a dive bar, but whenever our eyes met, we held each other's gaze ever-so-slightly longer than normal in a friendly interaction. He reached his leg out under the table and slowly began massaging my foot with his.

Our small group walked from the bar to a diner down the street and he reached for my hand and innocently held it, throwing the occasional smirk and a wink. At the diner, we continued our game of footsie. Mundane conversations evolved into more personal dialogue as we discussed the intricacies and nuance of queer sexualities. I was surprised when Drew revealed that he was also trans while discussing how our sexualities evolve as we grow and change as people. I felt a brief moment of jealousy. Although I had been living as a woman in many facets of my life for years, nobody was ever surprised to learn that my gender identity differed from what I was assigned at birth.

After we ate, four of us went back to my shoebox of a basement apartment—Drew, his roommate, my roommate, and me. We piled on the pullout bed in the living room, drinking beers and watching cartoons. Before I really knew what was happening, Drew kissed me. Our roommates kissed. After a few minutes, they went elsewhere.

I felt more nervous than I ever had before. I had been out as trans for years but I still hadn't had any sexual or romantic encounters with another trans person. And there I was on the sofa bed in my living room with the most attractive man I had ever met, a man who happened to also be trans. We undressed each other slowly and deliberately. Drew held me gently but securely. As he took my nipple into his mouth, waves of joy pulsed throughout every inch of my body. In all my experiences I had never felt anything quite like that. He took control in a way that was not dominant but confident and comforting.

We spent the next several hours exploring each other's bodies, affirming our own identities. Every time we touched, I felt the masculine leave my body, a wrong being righted. He climbed on top of me, gently kissing my neck and telling me how beautiful I was. With his weight on top of me, I felt my body transform from linebacker to ballerina. He held me closely as we rolled around the bed, unable to distinguish up from down as two people passionately became one.

If a stranger had seen us having sex, their description would be almost unrecognizable to us. An outside observer would say that I penetrated Drew, that I was the *man* and he was the *woman*.

But nothing could have been farther from the truth.

It felt as though our genitals had switched places. I felt like he was entering my body. For one brief night, I felt that the errors made in my mother's womb had been corrected. I had known intellectually that my womanhood could exist and be powerful regardless of what I had between my legs, but for the first time in my life, I truly felt that I was really a woman.

The next day we all went out for lunch at a nearby Tex-Mex restaurant. Drew and I sat next to each other, holding hands as we ate. After lunch, my roommate and I walked our guests back to their car. Drew kissed me and held me in an embrace that felt as though it would never end and then he and his roommate began their two-hour drive home. I hoped we would see each other again, but that was not meant to be. A few months later, we both moved to different cities a continent apart from each other.

Drew and I haven't spoken in almost four years, but few days go by where I do not think of him and of the beautiful night we shared. A girl never forgets the time she lost her virginity, even if that experience defies the definition as we know it.

Sex has the power to transform us. Being intimate can add connection to relationships, and it can also make us feel independent and powerful—

Look what I can do with my hands, my mouth.

Look how I can give you pleasure.

Look at me taking charge.

Sex can also bring us to a deeper understanding of who we are and what we need.

In the last story, Alex had to embrace her own identity before she could experience the kind of sex she wanted. In the next one, Chelsey's first-time sexual experience confirmed and celebrated what she knew to be her truest self.

{ Right now, I'm naked and lying **stomach-down**, my belly pushed into the green scratchy carpet of my bedroom floor. }

{ It's kinda like iced tea with a dash of salt. A vague, **sweet** sort of salty. }

{ And this is fun— a lot of fun! }

12

Ear Muffs for Muff Diving

Chelsey Clammer

I don't really notice any funky smell. And the taste isn't terrible, either. It's kinda like iced tea with a dash of salt. A vague, sweet sort of salty. My basketball teammates swore it was going to be all rotten and fishy down there. I don't get that. Why they would say vag is like rank tuna? Doesn't that mean they, too, smell like dead fish? Besides, none of them have ever dived into a muff as I am diving into a muff right now, so they don't know what they're talking about. Carpet muncher, they'll call me tomorrow. Jealous, I'll say. Because you can take my word for it, I've never before smelled nor tasted anything that's as full of life as this is. Though yesterday they did get me all afraid of what this was going to be like. And so, I feared my girlfriend's vagina would be a mucky swamp.

It is not.

Vagina smells like vagina.

Vagina tastes like vagina.

And I like it.

I don't know why I like it. I don't know why I'm only attracted to girls, not sure why I think dudes are gross. But the definition of gross, i.e., men, is not what I'm thinking about right now. Right now, I'm naked and lying stomach-down, my belly pushed into the green scratchy carpet of my bedroom floor. My head is between my girlfriend's legs and I'm finally having sex. Here's my tongue. Here's my girlfriend's vagina. Here's my tongue on my girlfriend's vagina and here I am having my first sexual experience. Ever. And it's awesome.

"But how do you *know* you're a lesbian?" Basketball teammates asked me yesterday. "You've never even had sex with a woman. How do you know that's what you want to do for the rest of your life?" I just knew. And, well, now I am having sex with a woman. And I was right. A proud dyke.

I'm licking my way to my identity.

I feel like a natural at this.

Courtney's pubic hair starts tickling the tip of my nose, which is about to make me sneeze. Fuck! That would suck! So I push my face further into her folds. Pressing my nose and mouth more into her, I can now feel her pubes on my tongue.

They don't taste gross either.

I don't know if it's my saliva or some sort of wet coming from Courtney's vagina, but I feel a liquid starting to spread across my lips and trickle down my chin. Then she moans. I must be doing something right.

With her feet on the floor and her knees bent over my shoulders, I loop my arms around her legs and hold on tight. My hands grab onto that soft area between the top of her thighs and the insides of them. It's so very grab-able. I'm in love with it already. I squeeze my arms around her legs like they're a harness slapped down on me for a roller coaster ride. Yes. I hold on for life.

My tongue separates the lips of her vagina and I find her clit with the tip of my tongue. At least I think it's her clit. It's this hard little ball thing. I press on it, and Courtney's legs start to quiver. I'm not quite sure what to do with my chin, so I push it closer to her, dig my chin a bit further past the fringe of her lips. She likes this. She moves her hips, riding my face like the horses she loves. Her hips are bucking.

Like I said, I'm a natural.

I explore. I unwrap my right arm from her thigh and stick two fingers inside of her. Wet, warm—could be called swamp-like—but only a swamp found in heaven! So welcoming. Mesmerizing. Lush. My fingers have found their place in the world. They were always supposed to be right there. My mouth, too. It's like I'm whispering a hidden language into her body, a language I'm finally letting myself speak.

I push my fingers further in, add a third, pump away. From her increasingly loud moans and heaving breathing, I know she feels good. The further in I go, the more it feels like I'm touching a part of myself, my identity revealed. Every second in her vagina, I am more and more a lesbian. I am myself.

And this is fun—a lot of fun!

A slightly-salty wet seeps out of her as she grabs onto my hair and squeezes my head with her legs like I'm one of Suzanne Sommers's ThighMasters. I'm having a harder time hearing her moans now. The sound is all muffled because now, with her legs squishing my ears into her inner-thigh flesh, I feel like I have ear muffs on for this muff-diving adventure. But even with muffled hearing, I can still hear some epic moans. And then she pushes her wet vag further into my face, gyrating. Well, this is the best activity, ever, though my jaw's starting to get a little sore and I'm losing some tongue strength. She's wearing me out.

But with my tongue on her clit and her body squirming about, all I can think of now is *I'm a lesbian! I'm a lesbian!* This realization is on a solid rotation in my head. It's all I can think about. Yes, now I'm an official lesbian. Hell yeah.

There's another big moan and some more hard hip thrashing and more of that thigh-squeezing and then soon her hands let go of my hair and my mouth lets go of her sex as she breathes heavily, her breath heaving her chest up and down. Up and down.

I sit up and wipe her salty liquid taste from my chin. A hair tickles the back of my throat. I pull it out and stare at—it's proof that I'm a lesbian. I kinda want to keep it.

Courtney smiles at me. "Mmm. Dessert." I imagine my chin is glistening like the fingers that were inside of her are glistening. Sparkling, even. I exhale, smile. Yes, lesbian.

Yes, that's me.

Two people can choose to have sex for no other reason than that it feels good. It doesn't have to be the next step in a committed relationship. It doesn't have to be about love. But if you tell me that it means nothing, I'll lift an eyebrow in disbelief. The essays in this book are proof enough. No matter how many years have passed, the writers remember vivid details about how it felt, what they thought, why they did it, and what it meant.

Sex can be about power or intimacy or relationship or rebellion or babies but we are a long way from a time in human evolutionary history where sex is for reproduction alone. That's why people have been writing books and telling jokes about sex for centuries.

It's also why, in the next story, Erica's first time is intricately connected to a much more complicated narrative about friendship and faith and finding our way.

{ **Dizzying** hours on his bed, the couch in his living room, my bed, other people's houses, parks. }

{ And we have sex and two minutes later it's over and I can't **believe** it. }

13

It Would Not Be an Overstatement to Say I Knew Nothing

Erica Lorraine Scheidt

Verse one

The first boy I ever slept with just tried to friend me on Facebook, but I didn't friend him back. I'm not saying this will happen to you. I'm not saying that the first boy you have sex with will grow up and have a sketchy profile picture and try to friend you in that way that people who Google their ex-girlfriends do when they're bored or horny. I'm not even saying that just because he's posing in front of a window covered with a make-shift curtain it necessarily means that he's a lonely guy living in a dingy apartment googling his ex-girlfriends. But it does make you wonder.

verse two

I'm one of the nobodies at my school. The girl who cries a lot. The girl with a big nose and a weird best friend. The girl who might be easy but who cares? I don't care. It's summer. School's out. Mel's doing my makeup. We're going downtown to the underage nightclub. We've been planning it for weeks. We have no idea what goes on there.

I have these stories about that time in my life. I tell them when I talk about dropping out of high school or my parents' divorce or why my teenage years unfolded the way they did. I think adolescence is this unbearable waiting until one day you go to a party or kiss another kid or take a drink of alcohol, and then—*all of a sudden* —it's like you're on a roller coaster. You want to remember every minute of that first kiss or that first party but then there's another and then another. Things happen, all kinds of things, and when it spits you out again you're twenty or twenty-two or twenty-six, and you can't remember actually choosing to get on that ride.

I have these stories about Mel and me, dreaming in the basements of our parents' homes, as though we would be these in-between people—these fourteen-year-old explosions waiting to happen—forever.

Mel's really good with makeup. She wears all the colors: silver-purple, purple, mauve, purply silver. Her own eyes have plum-colored eyeliner and purple mascara. Her glasses are superthick and have a pinkish-purple tinge. Her eyes are startlingly beautiful beneath, strangely large and brown and intelligent, full of all these bottomless things, unspoken. I have no patience for makeup, all the little brushes. I use my middle finger to apply plain brown eyeshadow to my lid. Mel takes over. She makes me sit still. She's "highlighting my brow bone," she says.

I have a new outfit. The skirt is a black cotton miniskirt, really straight with zippers all over it, and I have a yellow tank top and a red shirt made out of netting over that. The whole outfit is brand new, bought today at the Galleria by my mom. It's weird. She never does that. But I tried it on and she bought the whole outfit, right off the rack, not even on sale.

If you unzip the zippers, there's nothing underneath but skin.

The thing about downtown, the thing about living in the suburbs, is that nobody from our school will be there. Nobody at our school has even heard of the club. Mel and I could be anyone. And it's night and we're downtown and nobody knows that her mom dropped us off or my mom is picking us up or that I've never had an outfit like this and most of my clothes don't look anything like the girl I want to be.

It's strange, right? How well I remember that skirt, how I came out of the dressing room looking like a totally different girl and how, even now, the thing I remember the most is that pulsing longing to be seen, really seen, by my mom or my friends or by strangers, anyone. And while everything else has changed, this feeling has not.

verse three

It's a hot weekend night and the line outside the club winds around the corner. We feel good. Me in my zippered skirt. Mel all peaceful and smiling. I have three earrings in one ear and one in the other. Mel has even more.

And—Mel!

Shy Mel, starts talking to the boys behind us in line.

Zoom in.

They're smoking clove cigarettes. Mel's teasing them.

Now I'm the quiet one. I take the cigarette out of one of the boy's fingers and hold it in between my own. This will become my signature move. I will smoke this clove cigarette and then another. I will smoke cloves and then cigarettes. This is the inhale and exhale that foreshadow a decade of smoking and then a decade of quitting.

His name is Aaron and he has a big nose too. Not sharp like mine but flat and wide. We have the same haircut, short in the front and longer in the back.

I fill with the sweet, spicy smoke. A kind of recognition happens. We are two girls, and they are two boys, and we don't know anyone they know, and they don't know anyone we know. There's nothing to lose. It's the moment that separates everything that came before from everything that came after.

It's the summer night that I stepped, unknowing, onto the roller coaster. When I went from being the weird, big-nosed, oversensitive, bookworm girl with my weird, fuzzy-haired friend in weird, ill-fitting clothes—

—to the zippered miniskirt girl, dancing with this boy: his hips against mine, his hands seeking mine, his fingers brushing that part of my neck. This is exactly the way it was supposed to happen.

At the end of the night I lick my lips and the clove cigarettes leave a salty stain. Then he kisses me and I've been kissed before, but this is his mouth and my mouth and Duran Duran and Thompson Twins and Prince, and his fingers wrap around mine, and Mel is waiting with his friend until we are done. That night and the next morning when I close my eyes it's like a chill in my belly and along my skin, and I replay everything he said and everything I said, over and over, and how his breath felt on my neck when we were dancing.

The next day I ask my mom if I can go to the mall with Mel and when we do, he's there. Just like he said he would be.

I wish you could picture us. The mall. How nervous I was that he wouldn't show.

Fifteen-year-old Aaron is a Christian. His family is Christian. I've just joined a Christian youth group, but I haven't yet been born again. I write a lot in my spiritual journal. I worry about sin and temptation. I worry about scattering instead of gathering. I worry that I'm too clothes conscious, that I lie too easily, that I use suggestive language. I'm jealous, I note in my journal, of non-Christians and their parties. I've never been to a party.

And then this: suddenly I have a boyfriend. He comes to my church, and I go to his. My mom likes him. His parents like me. It's summer. There are movies and groping on the couch under the afghan. There's going to the mall and dancing and clove cigarettes. I take his jacket as a joke and he lets me keep it. He has a bottle of Jim Beam under his bed and porn magazines he stole from his father. I wear the jacket everywhere. At night he calls me on the phone, "I love you. I love you. I love you."

Aaron feels deeply. Love drives him crazy. He loves me so much he can't stand it. Often he does not sleep. He writes me letters in the middle of the night. They're about love and sex and God and boredom and drinking and the crushing weight of life. They're written on thin pieces of green paper. He carries around my picture.

He has pointy elbows, sparse black hairs on his chest. The soles of his feet are a different color. The chalky dryness of the skin on top of his knees. The bone above the arch of his foot. The place where his hair stops and there's just skin until his ear connects, the nape of his neck, even the word, nape. The long sweep of his body from his shoulders, down his back, down the back of his legs. The space between the cheeks of his ass and that pinching piece of skin under his balls and his balls, moving under all that wrinkly purple gray skin that changes from loose to taut.

And the laughing.

I'm fourteen, with my new body, and never have I been this aware, this intimate, with another person's body. Never have I felt before—startling, this!—some other person's folds.

His secret body. We are touching and kissing and laughing, and his hips and penis are pushing against my stomach, and we are laughing again.

It was all good, this. Touching the part of his fingertips where the nail met the skin. Feeling the swollen pads of his fingers.

I am the star of this story. Me as an object of desire. Me with a boyfriend. Me with a best friend. Me, me, me, me.

verse four
We're together anytime we can be, and there's everything between Aaron and me except penetration because we're Christian and fornicators will not inherit the Kingdom of God.

This makes it simple. Oral sex. Kissing. Aaron coming in his pants. Coming in my hand. Coming in my mouth. That's all okay. My mom and stepdad are gone a lot. His parents are gone a lot. There are marathon hours of *I want to but we can't* and all the things that feel good. His hands on me, my hands on him. Dizzying hours on his bed, the couch in his living room, my bed, other people's houses, parks. Before that night at the club, time stood still—everything breathing, waiting. Now everything balloons into a fever of letters and phone calls and his hand in mine.

When my mom and stepdad go away for the weekend and I'm supposed to be sleeping over at Mel's house, Aaron spends the night at my house, and we spend hours fooling around. Then we're in bed and the Bible is out and open on the bed, and we are reading and rereading passages and trying to find a work-around because we *do* want to inherit the Kingdom of God. We're talking and talking and talking, and then we have the dictionary out, and we're looking up *unrighteous* and *fornication*.

It's three in the morning.

I say, "Fuck it."

He says, "Literally?"

I say, "Yes."

And we have sex and two minutes later it's over and I can't believe it. It's not possible that *this* is fornication but Aaron says, "Let's do it again."

And we do.

After that, school starts. Aaron is moody and drinking and I don't get to see him very often. We only have sex every once in a while because it's getting harder to find time alone. I use the sponge as birth control, and it seems very modern because it's advertised in magazines, but it's sticky and difficult to take out. I'm never sure if I'm doing it right but I must be because I don't get pregnant, not until years later when I try the pullout method, which, it turns out, is not really a method of birth control at all.

verse five

Aaron says he's drunk when he sends me the letter: *I love you, Erica. I love you, Erica. I love you. I love you. I love you. I love you. I love you. I love you.* Hundreds of times in back-slanted scrawl on both sides of the green unlined paper, he writes *I love you*, darker in places where his pencil presses too hard.

verse six
Aaron and I stay together for a few more months, and I spend a lot of time talking about Aaron with his best friend Noah, and then Noah and I kiss, and I break up with Aaron. It's Christmas. Aaron sends me roses and a card that says, "It was just the two of us in one world, and now it's each of us in our own separate worlds." A few weeks later I break up with Noah and get back together with Aaron, but it's different now and doesn't last.

There's another boy after that, and I know I don't want to have sex with him but I don't know how to stop it once it starts. And it's hard to know what else to do when you have big empty swaths of time and you don't have anything you're moving toward. For me it's going to be writing, but I haven't figured that out yet.

Time speeds up. I stop going to church. Mel gets mono and misses almost a whole year of school and suddenly we're not friends anymore. I get a job at Sunshine Pizza and drop out of high school and start writing and start to feel like I'm good at something. I smoke a million cigarettes and read a million books and sleep with a million boys and I sleep with a girl and then another. I careen through depression and apartments and roommates and colleges and short stories. It's dizzying. I discover my own body and the pleasure it contains. I fall in love over and over in new ways.

Before, when I told the story of my first time, I always said that I dated this lovely boy and ours was a sweet, sweet love. But now when I reread Aaron's letters, I think that he was drinking far more than I understood. His was a different story, but I was so blinded by myself, by my hunger to be seen, I couldn't know him. And when he friended me last month, even though I didn't friend him back, I clicked around. He's still Christian, sober now, and I'm a lesbian with my own family, and I wish the story wrapped up in some neater way.

Aaron and I had all that. I'm talking about the joy. And then I kept looking for it again in a crush of bodies and emotions and urgency. But it wasn't until much later, with a woman, that I found that joy again. But maybe that's the way it works. Maybe I needed the crush and tangle of limbs and years to get here.

The first time.

We peel off clothes.

We slide toward naked, entering sex as if it were just us, just two people's bodies. Simple and uncomplicated. But we are rarely bare and unburdened. These bodies of ours— magnificent, strong, ripe—are often so deeply buried under outside and inside judgments that it can be hard to hear ourselves. It's easy to disconnect from the body and push its wants and needs below the surface.

For Kate, it took many years to unbraid her body from a complicated tangle of shame and silence.

14
How to Make a Braid
Kate Gray

*D*ivide *what you have into three equal sections. Grab the right section with your right hand and the left section with your left hand, letting the middle section hang free (for now).*

Shame is hard to hold in one hand, its gristle sharp and slimy at the same time. My mother is telling me not to walk that way, not to talk so loud. She's researching hormone treatments to stunt my growth because I'm five-feet-nine-inches tall in sixth grade and she's afraid I'll be a giant. My wrists stick beyond shirt-sleeves. My ankles stick below the legs of my pants. I know I don't fit the family. I'm different. I'm not right.

These are the messages I hold in one hand.

Hold tight.

What happens when breasts grow early is that other people notice, especially men. At parties, at the grocery store, at the post office in our small town, men touch my arm, crowd me in lines, carry my groceries. The town pediatrician squeezes my breasts for lumps when I am nine years old.

In the New England winter, the neighbors' garage becomes a movie house where I run the projector on "old movie night." The black-and-white actors walk on a distant screen, film clattering in the sprockets. At intermission I try to dodge the old men who circle the hors d'oeuvre table and try to touch my butt or brush against my braless breasts. When I mention the way the men act to my sisters, they say, "Oh, that's Mr. So-and-So," as if how long he's been misbehaving excuses him, as if I'm the one with the problem for saying something out loud.

In the left hand, hold silence, greasy and clotted. Let the middle section hang free (for now).

A girl at school changes the words to a camp song:
My Daddy lies over the ocean,
My Daddy lies over the sea,
My Daddy lies over my Mommy,
And that's what became of me.

When I get home that day, I chase my mother who is retreating into her office and sing it for her because my pubescent mind thinks the song clever. In the dim autumn light, her face drains like the painting called *The Scream*, and she turns around and walks away.

Her office door closes.

Rumor has it that an eighth-grade girl had an abortion. Other girls I know are sneaking out of their homes at night to meet boys. The mysteries of body and boy are beyond me. When I start my period at age eleven, my mother hands me a Kotex pamphlet about menstruation and never brings the topic up again. No one takes the time to have The Talk with me. There is no sex ed. No one in biology explains reproductive organs.

In biology class, when the teacher asks us to write what we feel about sex, he says, "Be honest." When I write, "The topic of sex embarrasses me," the teacher reads out loud what I've written, points me out, cannot contain his laugh. My hippie sister with long blond braids comes home from college and tells me to use tampons because they will help with sex. The blush on my face hides the gap in understanding.

Cross the left section over the middle section.

That middle section of the braid is my body.

At my all-girls boarding school I discover Want. Taller than most girls, more developed than many, with no men prowling to rub themselves on me, I grow into my body a little.

Before I am sixteen years old, I go home from boarding school for a weekend to help an old friend and his wife who have a new baby. During the night, this man stumbles into the room where I sleep, and he is drunk, and he kisses me, pouring his beer-sour breath into me, putting his big fingers into me, too. When his hand tries to open my legs wider, I push him away, and he moves away. When he leaves, I don't sleep. The irony keeps me awake—sweet sixteen and never been kissed. When the saying leaves my head, I wonder about men and fingers and hymens. I don't know if I'm a virgin anymore.

During the rest of high school, the middle section of the braid—my body—lifts to the top. I hug friends too long. I play varsity sports. One night two friends and I look for mischief and find the door unlocked to the old gym, and the girls and I lie on a stack of gymnastics mats and roll into each other and onto each other and never say a word.

A week before college starts, my mother drops me off to see the town pediatrician who no longer touches my breasts because a nurse is required to be in the room when I undress. He gives a speech about boys in college and how they drink and how, if they jump on top of me, I should "sit back and enjoy the ride." My mother and I do not speak when she picks me up from the doctor's office.

Between freshman and sophomore year of college, I ride a train to Arizona to become a counselor at a horse camp. At eighteen years old I've never been to a camp, been a counselor, or seen the desert. Horses scare me. The first night the assistant director, whose camp name is Lizard, stands up to welcome everyone, and I think, "That is the ugliest woman I've ever seen." My body cringes.

By the third night in the Arizona mountains, I am freezing because I assumed Arizona would be hot and only brought shorts and T-shirts. Lizard and I meet late at night outdoors, which is very dark and dangerous. (New England doesn't have mountain lions, bears, scorpions, tarantulas. Arizona does.) For the first time in my life, my body tops my mind. The cringe of a few days ago turns to jitters in Lizard's presence, her overt desire, her lean twenty-four-year-old body.

Lizard puts her arm around me, and when her skin meets my skin, I feel the earth open up and welcome me as part of all creation. I connect with stars and planets and space. When she kisses me, I'm equally sure that I will grow warts, turn green, and burn in hell.

That weekend she takes me to a hotel in town.

Continue braiding the three strands.

When we drive up to the hotel to get a room, Lizard tells me to duck in my seat so the manager can't see me. Two young women renting a room is suspect. Homosexuality in Arizona at the time is a crime. Two girls who are one planet, all body and Want, are in danger. She gets the room. We drive around back, and Lizard goes in without me.

Sneaking is part of the strand that was once in my left hand—*silence.*

When I go to the door and open it, smoke and sour carpet and Lysol hit me. Lizard's hands pull me in, and her hands and my hands fill with shirts and zippers and skin. My lips are full of lips and fingers and the sinew of her neck. The curtains are closed, and we draw the grimy cover off one bed and fall into it. We have no clothes. I have never felt the long, lean body of someone else on my long, lean body, skin-to-skin, hands all over. When her hand reaches into me, her fingers find spots I didn't know I had—places of silence and rumor and old-movie innuendo, the place my sister said tampons should go.

I'm sure I will go supernova.

We don't sleep. Her fingers are in me. My fingers are in her. My tongue tastes her salt. Her tongue tastes my salt. At times I'm not sure which breast is hers and which is mine, and I don't know what is happening. I have no frame of reference from book, movie, or rumor. Fred Astaire and Ginger Rogers are black-and-white dancers, and this dance is color and grit and girl.

In the morning the edges of the smelly curtains let light in, and the wall-size mirror facing the bed shows bare legs and shoulders and messed-up hair. The room is full of smoke and sour carpet and Lysol and sex. The bathroom is across the room and to get there means crossing in front of the mirror and that means seeing my body so I crawl under the mirror to avoid it. My body is wrong.

In the bathroom I shut the door, and I sit on the toilet, and I think, "What is happening?" I have no answer. When I walk out of the bathroom, Lizard has the light on, and I ask her to turn it off. In the dark, our bodies are a little more right than wrong, and somehow skin touching skin soothes the friction of the sin I believe I'm committing. We spend the day in bed. By the time we return to camp that evening, I can barely walk I am so sore.

By the end of the summer, the camp counselors and the camp administration have split over the issue of counselors loving counselors. I am an outsider, an East Coast girl, and I am blamed for corrupting the camp. Lizard drives me from Arizona to Connecticut and drops me off.

Tie the braid tight.
Silence braids into shame and body.

It takes years to realize that I lost my virginity. All those long winters of growing up, with movie reels turning and the films clicking through the projector, I learned what virginity was and wasn't in black-and-white. I thought losing virginity required a penis and penetration and blood and the back seat of a Chevy, so I don't connect fingers and tongues and fists and clitoris and vagina to a summer of dark hotel rooms and secret meetings and sex between girls.

It takes years to recognize the loss and the gain, the rite of passage, the murky way my body expressed Want. It takes many more years before I untie that braid and finally stand in front of a mirror to see my long, lean body, naked.

Maybe you're the romantic type—

Sex is going to be magical, wild, fireworks! The two of us will be together forever.

Maybe you're more cynical—

It's going to hurt. This is the only way to keep my guy interested. Let's just get it over with.

Or maybe you're practical—

This sex thing is no big deal. It couldn't be harder than driving a car. I've got this.

Whatever your attitude, whether you're focused on having fun or deepening a relationship, what matters most is sexual agency. You get to decide what happens. It's up to you when you have sex and why you have sex. Every kiss, every touch, every time.

Justina thought about what she wanted. She laid down her ground rules. And when opportunity presented itself, she got down to business.

15

Me, Some Random Guy, and the Army of Darkness

Justina Ireland

This is the story of the first time I had sex in all of its awkward, poorly planned glory. But before I tell you about it I should probably tell you this: I never thought my first time would be special.

Actually, that's not *entirely* true. When I was younger, too young to really get the sexy scenes in R-rated movies but too old for Disney princesses, I did believe my first times would be special: first date, first kiss, first whatever came next. Can you blame me? When you think there are faraway lands filled with talking animals, it's easy to believe that some special guy will rescue you from your craptastic life.

As I got older, reality chipped away at the fantasy. My first kiss was from a guy that had just smoked his weight in marijuana and tasted like Doritos and cotton mouth. My first date was walking around the mall with a guy who was just using me to get close to my friend, since everyone knew she was a sure thing. And even though I hadn't had sex, I'd heard about plenty of terrible, awful, heartbreaking first times.

All of my friends seemed to be having sex and their secondhand accounts didn't exactly make me want to declare myself open for business, so to speak. If their story wasn't about someone walking in, then it was about how much it hurt, felt weird, or just generally sucked, especially when they found out they'd gotten the gift that keeps on giving (*herpes!*). Sex was generally terrifying, first-time sex even more so.

And the girls who did have a wonderful first time weren't convincing me to get naked with some guy, either. Their stories reeked of self-delusion. Experience had taught me that teenage boys did not have the sensitivity and consideration I'd come to expect from a life spent reading romance novels. No boy was going to suddenly turn into Prince Charming once his pants were down, no matter what some girls would tell you.

So when it came to sex I was pretty cynical about the whole thing. Expectations of rose petals and soft music changed to a bed and a condom. That's right. My ground rules for my sexual debut were:

Rule #1: It had to happen in a bed. No cars, no bathrooms, no couches. I wanted a bedroom and a locked door, dammit. No one's little brother was going to walk in while I was sprawled on a bed with my hooty-hoo bared to the world.

Rule #2: I was not getting knocked up, and chlamydia just sounded gross, so that meant there had to be protection. I wasn't going to go on birth control pills because they were expensive, and besides, the thought of oozing sores (*oozing sores!*) on my muffin was mentally paralyzing. That meant the guy had to have a condom. If I was going to invite someone into my lady business, the least they could do was wrap it up. No exceptions. I was not going to end up a statistic.

And that was it. It had to be clean and private. I didn't think that was too much to ask.

But . . . it was. My ground rules were a little too ambitious, it seemed. And it's really hard to expect too much after your best friend tells you about losing her virginity in the bathroom of a fast-food restaurant.

Even if my standards were low they were still standards. I was putting myself first, in a way. However, I wasn't holding out for having my world rocked or really much fun at all. I'd explored my hidden valley often enough that I knew what felt good, and none of the fumbly-handed interactions I'd had with boys came close. If I wasn't going to end up with an orgasm I *definitely* wasn't going to end up someone's mommy or a viral incubator. Boys who wanted in my pants had to meet my standards. Otherwise I was out.

I made it through high school and into the United States Army a card-carrying member of the V club. It wasn't something I really thought much about, to be honest. I mean, I thought about sex, but any sexy daydreams were quickly ruined by the thought of the guys that usually liked me: broke, shiftless, selfish. These guys didn't work and called every girl they knew a bitch or a slut. There were some real peaches playing in my league and I'd found every single one of them.

Daydreams were only safe if I thought about having sex with someone I didn't know and would never meet, like movie stars. I can't tell you how many times I surrendered to passion in Leonardo DiCaprio's capable arms. Or, you know, Kate Winslet's. My fantasies weren't picky. But that just made the reality of sex seem even further away. It was a catch-22: I didn't have sex because I couldn't find a decent guy, but I didn't find a decent guy because I wasn't really all that concerned about having sex.

But all of that was before I went to language school at the Defense Language Institute, DLI for short, in beautiful Monterey, California.

Monterey was the first place where I was really on my own. No curfew, no mom asking prying questions, no anyone. There were no rules at DLI save the ones the Army enforced, and those were flexible enough that I was finally able to feel alive. If I wanted to eat my weight in chocolate cake (and I did, who wouldn't?) then I could. I could stay up all night watching bad television and roll out to class early the next morning, bleary-eyed and rumpled. There was no one to influence my choices, and no one to warn me about bad decisions. The only person responsible for me was me, and I was more intent on having fun than using good judgment.

It was a great time to have some ill-advised nooky.

Although sex was not my first thought when I arrived in Monterey it quickly became a priority. In a place where random hookups were the norm, being a virgin was a hassle. It was the social equivalent of having a nine o'clock curfew. People I was serving with were either college graduates or had lived on their own before join-ing the military. They'd had sex. Lots of sex. Cringe-worthy and swoon-worthy and just plain worthy sex. They had funny stories about sex gone wrong and horror stories of why you never want to have sex in the Atlantic Ocean at night (*jellyfish!*). I laughed at these stories and I nodded when appropriate but I never shared any of my own escapades.

Um, because I didn't *have* any.

I was the youngest in my platoon and underage, so I was already excluded from the barhopping that comprised most social outings. I didn't have a college degree and I had no stories about "the one that got away" to wistfully recall.

But being a virgin?

That marked me as a kid like nothing else.

When sex talk came up and it was revealed, usually by someone else, that I'd never had sex, that's when the head pats began. I was an adorable little kitten to be sheltered and protected. Being a vir-gin became an indicator of just how much I hadn't lived, that I was completely inexperienced.

And it was annoying as fuck.

So I set out to get laid because somehow I figured that was going to fix the *Oh, aren't you just adorable?* attitude people took toward me. I could be one of *those girls* or I could be a child, and being one of *those girls* was preferable. But I was going to be one of those girls in a room with a locked door, a bed, and protection. Those were still nonnegotiable.

I learned quickly that guys are not necessarily eager to do it with everyone's favorite little sister, which is what I'd become. No one wanted to deflower me because they liked me too much. They respected me too much.

Mostly they were terrified of my expectations.

"Virgins are a hassle," one male friend told me. "They want flowers and special moments, and none of the other girls are expecting that kind of thing. They already know the deal. No one has to worry about them falling in love after hooking up, you know?"

But I didn't know. *Because no one would have sex with me!*

I had a couple of close calls, but there was always something to ruin it (roommates walking in, lack of a condom). After nearly a year I'd given up on ever doing it. Life seemed determined to keep me celibate forever.

I started to formulate these insane plans for how I was going to get laid. They were just as sad as they were impossible. I imagined approaching a male prostitute, assuming I could find one, and shoving a handful of dollars at him. Once I told him what I wanted he'd say, "Wait, you're a virgin? Oh sweetie, no. Just . . . no." Then he'd pat me on the shoulder, the kind of awkward tap you give someone when they've just had an elderly relative die, before he walked away.

Even in my imagination I was trapped in virginhood.

So, after nearly a year of trying to find a coconspirator, I stopped looking for one. And I focused on having fun. Meaning I started smoking and drinking heavily because that is how you spell fun when you're nineteen and not having sex.

And being deliriously, gloriously drunk is how I finally got laid.

I was at a house party where I was supposed to hook up with some guy who liked me but that I didn't know that well. Instead he decided to go after someone blonder and cuter, and I was a little crushed. Mostly because he'd been described as a sure thing, and even though I *wasn't* looking, I still wanted to chuck my V card out the window.

Rejection stinks, especially when you think you're going to get some sex and it doesn't happen. So once the sure thing started making out with the blond girl, I headed outside to babysit the keg.

If you're socially awkward and don't know anyone and are slightly embarrassed because a boy you sort of like is making out with a girl you don't know in the living room while everyone watches, the keg is the absolute best place to be. First, there's beer. Unlimited beer. Second, it's the social hub of any party. Everyone comes to visit the keg. Everyone. Even the people who prefer to pickle their liver with bottom shelf vodka that could double as paint remover.

Everyone visits the keg.

So I hung out and drank and laughed and drank and smoked and drank and joked around with people I didn't know while drinking some more. This was not the best idea I've ever had, because in general getting very, very drunk at a party is a recipe for disaster. I knew this firsthand from an incident at a previous party that had almost ended very badly for me. Due to a friend's timely intervention I didn't get raped, but unfortunately I was not so good at learning my lesson the first time.

So I started drinking more beer than I could handle. I was awkward and lonely and maybe just a little heartsore at being rejected. Not good reasons to drink to annihilation, but my reasons all the same.

In a stupidly short amount of time I was absolutely wasted.

Since I was too young to be drinking and too drunk to stand, I casually leaned myself against the side of the house, like I was cool and nonchalant and not completely shit-faced. I had just about convinced myself that I was not going to puke when a guy whose name I can't remember (It started with an M. Morgan? Morris? Mitch? Let's just go with Mitch.) came up and started talking about something (Music? Movies?). I nodded and laughed at the appropriate pauses, and he refilled my beer for me like a fine gentleman bartender. After a beer and a half he asked me if I wanted to go back to his place and watch movies.

I said, "Sure." Or, at least, I think I said sure. I'm positive whatever I slurred out was a pale imitation of English.

Now, on any other night I probably would've declined. After all, I still had my two rules (*Bed! Condom!*) and I'd arrived with a friend. It felt weird to leave with someone besides the people I came with, like it was a sordid tryst or a drug deal. More importantly, I would've realized that "going back to his room to watch movies" was code for having sex, and I would've been so freaked out about it that I would've stammered out some excuse and bolted.

And maybe I would've realized that a guy who gets a girl drunk before trying to nail her is a complete and utter shitbag.

But I didn't. I was drunk, my inhibitions were gone, and my decision-making skills were terrible. Besides, he was cute. I think. I was pretty much seeing double.

After waving off my concerned friend—*Yes, I'm good. I'm fine. Everything is fine.*—we went back to his room and locked the door. (Rule #1? Check.) He let me pick the movie and I chose *Army of Darkness*. Not just because I really like that movie but because his DVD collection was alphabetized and it was just too hard to keep reading past the As.

As Bruce Campbell, the star of the movie, drove his car through a portal into the past, the guy I was with reached up under my shirt. It wasn't the first time I'd imagined Ash, Bruce Campbell's character in the movie, reaching up under my shirt. But this time, it was really happening. Only, not with Ash, but with Mitch. I laughed at the silliness of making out to a movie that had fueled my own sordid daydreams.

But Mitch didn't know any of this, and he thought I was giggling at him. When he asked me if I was ticklish I told him the sad, sad truth: I was a virgin, untried and unproven. Instead of that turning him off, it actually turned him on.

Because he was a dirtbag.

I have to interject a note of caution here: Guys that are completely okay screwing girls too drunk to give enthusiastic consent are the lowest of the low. There is something loathsome about a guy that hits on a girl who is leaning against a house because she is too inebriated to stand. Those guys should be avoided at *all* costs.

Especially if the idea of being your first makes them hard.

But I was drunk, lonely, and a little desperate to have sex. I doubt any earnest warning would have been enough to scare off my nineteen-year-old self. I wanted to have sex even if the guy I'd picked wasn't really worth my time.

My sexual debut, with the movie playing in the background and me trying not to puke up a pony keg's worth of light beer while I fucked a complete stranger, was not my finest moment. But I'm glad I did it, even if I do have one regret.

I was totally off my game that night.

Anything worth doing should be done well, especially sex. Alcohol may lower inhibitions but it sure as hell doesn't increase coordination. My kissing technique had devolved into something between a garter snake doing an interpretive dance and a sea anemone slap fight. I had no idea what to do with my mouth. I pretty much totally forgot I even had hands. It all just seemed like too much effort to even try. By the time Mitch went down on me I really just wanted him to take off his pants and get down to business so I could pass out properly.

You know, because I was *shit-faced*.

He slid a condom on. (Rule #2? Check.)

And, dammit, I was finally doing it.

And it, the sex, well, it was pretty uninspired. Definitely less interesting than *Army of Darkness*.

Eventually he finished (I didn't. No surprise there.) and pulled me into his arms while he murmured bullshit platitudes for my newly deflowered benefit. I fell asleep. (Passed out. Whatever.)

The next morning I woke up at the ass crack of dawn. I've always been an early riser and sharing a twin bed with a guy I barely knew was not my idea of romantic. I used the bathroom, noted the soreness in my lady bits, and gave myself a high five.

Yay me. I'd done it!

As I was searching for my other shoe, Mitch woke up and asked me if I wanted to go to breakfast. No, I didn't. I wanted a hot shower and another twelve hours of sleep in my own bed. Besides, he was a lot less cute when I was mostly sober and it was light out. He asked for my number, and I gave it to him out of some strange sense of misplaced guilt. He called me the next weekend so that we could hook up again. But it was pretty terrible and I was glad I'd been so very drunk the first time. I was relieved when I saw him making out with someone else a month later, ending our awkward, half-hearted courtship.

And that is the somewhat sordid story of my forgettable first time.

I like to think I used Mitch as much as he used me. I'm not really sure. Because what I remember is being really, really drunk. And horny. And more than a little desperate to have sex.

But I also remember 1990s Bruce Campbell, the star of *Army of Darkness*.

He was hot.

After hearing her friend's story of sex in the bathroom of a fast-food restaurant, Justina didn't have very high expectations for her own first time, and it played out more or less to expectation. Not the greatest show on earth, but she knew what she was getting into. She had sex on her own terms.

As the stories in this book show, first-time sex isn't a one-size-fits-all proposition. We bring our expectations, experiences, and beliefs into bed with us. Sometimes sex is a letdown. Sometimes it's transformative. Sometimes it's a hell of a lot of fun. The key is figuring out what you want and asking for it.

Jamia isn't looking for sex when she goes to the beach with a friend, but she unexpectedly finds herself in a safe place with a sexy guy who is ready and willing to give her exactly what she desires, as she figures it out a little bit at a time.

{ Emboldened by the insistence of my own sexual energy, I felt **powerful** rather than fearful . . . . }

{ I was testing my limits, and they felt and tasted like **freedom**. }

{ . . . we lay in bed **discovering** each other and, most of all, discovering ourselves. }

{ . . . the tension that had been welling up inside me melted away. }

16

My Name Is Jamia

Jamia Wilson

"Hello, welcome to the Virgin Vault. How may I direct your call?"

When the communal phone rang in my all-girls boarding school dorm, we sometimes answered with the snarky name kids from other schools teased us with at sporting events. Peals of laughter would reverberate through the halls of the so-called Virgin Vault as we frustrated callers attempting to reach their sister, daughter, or friend.

When we weren't in class, this sort of innocent mischief imbued our days with a sense of rebellion. Joyful defiance was a way to temper our highly structured schedules, rigorous academic load, and extracurricular commitments.

Most days, deeply diving into my coursework, writing, and singing thrilled me. But sometimes, gripped with cabin fever, I would wonder why I was living with one hundred and twenty teen girls instead of following Lenny Kravitz's band on tour.

At the end of junior year, my friend Maureena (aka Mo) sauntered by me in study hall, interrupting business as usual at my desk.

I welcomed the distraction. Using her long blond hair as a shield, she dropped a tiny folded note in my lap.

Risking demerits by reading her message, I pretended to be immersed in a close reading of *The Awakening* while attempting to avoid the proctor's gaze.

While reading Chopin's novel about a young woman's sexual discovery would have usually been a highlight during study hours, the contents of Mo's note were more intriguing. I devoured her artful scrawl without a clue that it would lead to my very own awakening a month later.

When Mo wasn't at school, she lived with her grandfather at the beach. She often went home for weekends while I was stuck at school because my parents lived in Saudi Arabia. We'd been talking for months about me going home with her some weekend, and I couldn't wait.

As I suspected, Mo's letter was about our trip. Her note instructed me to request a letter from my parents authorizing the sleepover. She said our trip would be low-key. We'd stay at her grandpa's home, hang out with her friends at the beach, and I'd finally get to meet the cute college-aged boyfriend she kept gushing about.

In compliance with school policy, Mo's grandfather wrote a letter to our dean stating that he would be hosting us for a weekend break in the beginning of May. He left the note open-ended, welcoming me any time. We finally received the permission form from my parents and we were ready to go!

The day finally came and I eagerly waited for Mo's grandfather to retrieve us from campus. Adorned in her uniform plaid kilt and gray cardigan, Mo epitomized boarding school chic as she ran up to meet me at the main building. Her lean frame, strong jaw, and long blond hair reminded me of an Abercrombie & Fitch ad.

"There's been a change of plans," she said. Mo indicated a tall forty-something brunette standing next to a car. "Grandpa's tied up and running late. Jodie's mom is going to give us a ride instead."

I looked at the main office nervously and asked Mo if we needed new paperwork authorizing us to be driven by another adult. She grabbed my hand and said, "Don't worry. Everything is taken care of."

Two hours later, Jodie's mom left us at a Walmart near the beach. According to Mo, her grandfather wanted us to wait there for him to arrive. After assuring Jodie's mom that we would call her once we reached home, our chaperone departed.

Ten minutes later, Mo's boyfriend, Ben, and his friend, Steven, pulled up in an early-90s jalopy and whisked us off to what looked like a ramshackle frat house. When I asked when her grandfather was coming, Mo and her punk-rock paramour laughed in unison. "Sweetie," she said, "My grandpa is in Europe. I knew you wouldn't come if I told you what was up. It's just us, Ben, and his boys."

My gut churned with fear. We'd already violated school policy by riding in a car with unauthorized boys. Now we would be spending the weekend without parental guidance.

One by one, I visualized the privileges that would be taken away at school if our prefect or worse, the headmistress, learned that we broke the rules. I imagined sitting in a disciplinary council meeting and being punished for violating the honor code. If I got kicked out of school, I would spend the remainder of my life at a soul-sucking retail job. There was no way out without calling school, blaming Mo, and losing a friend. None of the options were appealing. We were in too deep by school standards already.

So I took a breath, and we entered the house. After all, I was almost a "grown-ass woman." I often proclaimed this phrase while posturing with my girlfriends about how we deserved more freedom at school, but now, facing a weekend of potential debauchery that could get me in huge trouble, I felt like a scared child.

In preparation for our arrival, Ben had organized a small gathering with pizzas, beer, tequila, and bro-punk music blaring throughout the house. I was sitting in one of those party atmospheres I'd seen a lot on television but wasn't entirely used to since the dynamics of the social scene in Saudi Arabia were very different.

For the first hour, I sat silently on a dusty couch as Mo chatted with friends from home.

As soon as I digested the fact that I had nowhere to go without getting Mo and possibly myself suspended—or even expelled—I decided to mingle. I learned that Steven was in college about twenty miles from our school, and Mo's boyfriend was working and applying to art school. Mostly, I observed aspects of '90s American teenage culture that I'd missed due to my expat lifestyle. Flip-cup and beer pong hadn't made it to the Middle East.

After most of the guests cleared out around midnight Mo began playing Hacky-Sack with Ben and Steven while I watched. My panic rose again. Not only was I violating policy before college applications and recommendations were complete, but I was also putting myself in a position where my lack of coordination was about to be revealed in front of handsome college boys.

Steven, who was tall with short brown curls and a kindly grin, kicked the Hacky Sack in the air toward me and winked. I summoned every ounce of dexterity I had to ensure that the darn little beanbag never hit the ground. To my amazement and triumph I grabbed it in midair, and then stood in awkward silence when I realized that I had ended the game.

As if on cue, Mo yawned and said it was time for her and Ben to go to bed. She wrapped her arms around his bony waist and led him toward the bedroom. Panicked, I asked where I should sleep, and she said Steven would show me where to go. Before I realized that the only other bed in the house was in Steven's room, he led me to the kitchen.

"Mia," he said. "Do you want something to drink? I noticed you haven't had anything since you've been here."

The last thing I wanted was to break more rules so I stammered, "I'm fine. Thank you. I don't really drink. Um, alcohol that is."

I added to the awkwardness by saying, "By the way, Mia is only what people I'm close to call me, you know like my best friends and my family. By the way, why do white people always want to shorten my name without permission? Jamia is phonetic. It's not that hard."

Laughing nervously, Steven asked me if I was okay with him drinking, and when I said I was, he helped himself to some tequila. I was sure his interest in me would evaporate, but instead he set his glass down and said, "Well, I hope to become one of those people who earns the right to call you by your nickname someday."

I feigned indifference. "Um . . . sure, do what you want. I mean, about the drinking, not the name."

The next twenty minutes seemed like an hour of awkward small talk until we both realized how quiet the house had become. The music stopped playing. Raindrops pounded on the roof. Sheet lighting cut the sky.

In silence, we watched the storm swirl past the kitchen window. Steven drank his tequila, and I prepared mint tea that I'd brought in my purse.

I sat on the washing machine in the kitchen because it was the only clean surface left after the party. Steven pushed a discarded pizza box over to make room for himself beside me.

"I've been watching you," he said. "I really like that you're kind of a hippie girl even though you don't really look the part. It's cute that you brought your own tea, Jamia. And please note, I'm no longer calling you Mia."

Feeling like myself for the first time that night, I said, "Yep, mint tea is my thing. It reminds me of being in Saudi Arabia where I grew up. It's kind of my comfort zone."

As I bent my head down to take another sip, he put his tequila down and grabbed my cup. Before I could protest, he removed it from my lips and placed it at his own.

I studied his face as he closed his eyes, took in the aroma and then allowed his face to be bathed by steam. He sipped my tea slowly and nodded with appreciation. His eyelashes were gorgeous and his lips were luscious. I realized that I'd just begun to see him clearly and wondered how he was seeing me.

He handed back my tea, apologizing for drinking so much of it. As I assured him that there was more than enough for us both, I leaned in to have another sip. Then he reached for my hair and tucked a loose curl behind my ear before it could fall into the hot water. As he stroked my face, I shivered and shifted in my seat, unsure how to deal with my increasing attraction.

Steven lifted my chin and gazed into my eyes until I blinked. I don't really remember exactly what happened next except that he slowly leaned in and kissed me behind my neck, and the tension that had been welling up inside me melted away. We kissed tenderly for what felt like hours. We knocked over the now-cold tea and soaked our clothes.

Steven asked if he could pour the rest of his tequila over me since we were already soaked from the tea. It was funny and, admittedly, somewhat awkward. It seemed so cliché, but I went with it as a rite of passage.

Steven poured the tequila slowly and proceeded to lick it off my neck and chest. My toes curled tightly as he trailed a salt-soaked finger down the sides of my neck and licked that off with a slow and sensuous pace. This set off a chain reaction of deep kissing and electrifying biting that left both of our necks looking like a red map of erogenous evidence.

Before this moment, I had been kissed twice, and once someone had touched my breast under my shirt for five seconds at a middle school party. This was a whole new frontier with fresh terrain to navigate and negotiate. I was testing my limits, and they felt and tasted like freedom.

I was far away from the daily ennui of study hall at the Virgin Vault. Always one to find a way back to my Protestant guilt, I shuddered a bit about what the chaplain and headmistress would say if my indiscretion got out and I prayed for forgiveness.

But while in the throes of passion . . . .

When Steven unbuttoned my jeans and took off my favorite purple shirt, my spine tingled. I wanted more and I chose to embrace it. Instead of showering myself in shame, I decided to give in to my desires despite my fear of punishment. I shoved away thoughts of the headmistress and turned down the volume of the voice of external authority in my head. I was in command now, and I sure as hell didn't want to stop.

Our make-out session progressed into the night, and our amorous movements accidentally turned on the washing machine. Laughing, we scrambled to turn it off before we woke up Mo and Ben. The kitchen really wasn't working for us.

Steven suggested that we head to his room. He must have seen the apprehension in my eyes because he said, "You're in charge of everything that happens in there. Nothing will happen that you don't want."

Relieved that I could continue with our exploration without committing to going all the way, I retreated into his room with him. Before the door closed, I told him that I wasn't ready to have sex but that I wanted to explore each other's bodies completely.

He asked me what I wanted, and I said that I wished to be kissed all over from head-to-toe with no expectations of anything coming of it, unless of course, it did.

He was happy to comply. The entire next day we lay in bed discovering each other and, most of all, discovering ourselves. The tightrope between our distance and our closeness led to a vulnerability that set the stage for me to experience my first (and explosively remarkable) orgasm.

And my second.

And my third.

This was not how I imagined my first sexual experience would be or with whom I thought it would be. There's no way I could have anticipated that I'd end up sharing everything from scar stories to sweaty embraces with a dude-bro on a tiny twin bed, with trip-hop music on in the background, and the scent of patchouli and mint tea in the air.

For one of the first times in my overthinking life, I felt fully embodied. I had skin. I had a body. I was giving in to cravings and I was devouring the succulence of release.

Emboldened by the insistence of my own sexual energy, I felt powerful rather than fearful or sinful like I'd been conditioned to believe in church and school.

Mo and I never ended up going to the beach. We were too nervous we would be spotted by people from school who might report our whereabouts to the administration. But the heavens were in on our little conspiracy of desire because rain soaked the town for the entire weekend.

We were confined to a house with two cute guys and nothing but music, pizza, and hormones to focus on. So that's what we did. And we never got caught.

Steven and I went our separate ways a few months later. I cut him off after hearing that he'd had sex with a girl from my high school during another one of Mo's sleepovers. He continued to pursue me but I realized that I was no longer interested in a college dude that hooked up with high school girls in the first place.

What's more, I wasn't ready to go all the way yet and was perfectly content waiting to go full throttle with someone I could truly trust. Even though my friends didn't believe me when I said it, I wasn't that upset when it didn't work out between Steven and me. The experience was never about him, it was about me learning to embrace my sexuality without fear. It was about being present in my body and enjoying the delicious fire of my humanity, my femininity, and my spirituality all at once.

I read that Judy Blume was inspired to write *Forever*, a candid and controversial novel about teen sexuality, because she had heard from teen girls who wanted to read a book about two teens who have sex and nothing bad happens to them. Even though Steven and I didn't "seal the deal," he will always be a part of my "Forever"

story because I learned that I could express healthy sexuality without damnation or losing myself. I was grateful for his gentle touch,
his affirmation of my idiosyncrasies, and for helping me to learn to
receive pleasure without guilt—okay, with minimal guilt.

Years later, I studied abroad in Italy, and over cappuccinos in
Campo Dei Fiori, I met a girl from Mo's small town. My mouth
dropped open.

"Small world. Do you know Steven S—, by chance?" I inquired,
innocently.

When she exclaimed that he was, in fact, her best friend from
high school, I couldn't believe it. I tried to play it cool because I
didn't want to risk her asking him about me.

As I contemplated what to say next, she said, "Oh, wait! *You're*
Mia! Mia? Wow! I heard you had a special experience together.
Weren't you also the one who wouldn't let him call you by your
nickname?"

I flashed her a sly smile.

"Yes, that's right. That's me."

Sex is not everything.

It's not a to-do list. There's no box for you to check, no V card to punch. You don't have to have sex, and if you do, it's just one part of the rest of your world. What I hope for you is that—when you're ready—sex and intimacy and closeness become a rich and wonderful part of your life.

So for now, don't worry about it.

Find your passions. Work hard. Take care of yourself. Play to your strengths. Be creative. Act according to your values. Surround yourself with good people. Be compassionate.

And above all—

Choose for yourself.

{ The air was thick and warm, sweet and still. My skin flushed. Tingled. }

{ When we stopped to catch our breath from giggling, we leaned into one another and kissed. }

{ He fumbled taking my bra off—the clasps a challenge for a rookie —and we lay chest to chest. }

17

It's All in the Choosing

Kelly Jensen

I never envisioned myself having sex.

I never dated in high school, was never truly kissed. I'd masturbated and was familiar with my body, but sex with another person wasn't something I thought I'd have to make a choice about doing. I had no idea how it might look or taste or feel even though I'd thought about it.

It wasn't that the idea of sex scared me. The opportunity just hadn't come up. I didn't find myself sexually attracted to anyone, and I didn't think I was sexually attractive. I was a girl with less-than-perfect skin and big boobs that didn't come with a thin or good-looking body. Years of being told I was fat and ugly grew beneath my skin and became how I saw myself.

It was how I imagined other people saw me, too.

During high school, I grew close to a boy I'd never met. We'd talked online and by phone, sharing pieces of ourselves we didn't share with anyone else. There was something connecting us— warm and gentle and soft—but making a commitment to one another when we didn't know if our rhythms would sync didn't make sense. We agreed that if things were meant to be they would work out.

The transition from home to my small college was tough. I didn't get along with my roommate and disliked my studies. I was lonely, even though I was almost never alone. I stole quiet time when I could to go out to the train bridge across campus. The wooden bridge, built over railroad tracks, connected the far edge of campus to the most rural parts of town.

Despite the rocky start, I soon met people who would become my closest friends. A group of us hung out every night on the landing connecting the all-male and all-female dorms. We'd stay up until the early hours of the morning talking about classes, our peers, what we thought about news or politics.

And, inevitably, we talked a lot about sex: whether we'd had it or not, whether we wanted to have it, who we'd love to have it with, logistics and expectations of every flavor. Even though I was one of the only virgins, I kept a jar of condoms in my room in case a friend needed one. Less embarrassing than going to the nurse or the RA.

One night, after pouring my heart out about how much I hated anthropology and dreaded doing any classwork related to it, a friend made me an offer: study and do well on my upcoming test, and he'd come by and we'd have sex. No pressure or commitment other than to enjoy myself.

I knew and trusted him, even though—or maybe because—he was open about his extensive sexual experiences. If I was going to have sex, it should be with someone who was that eager about having sex with me. With him, I figured it would be fun for fun's sake. If I didn't take the chance, would I see it again?

I did well on the test.

Before he came to my room on an afternoon neither of us had class, I put a condom in easy reach of my bed and wore a tank and shorts to be comfortable. Shaved. Having a plan made me less nervous. This was what we were going to do.

He and I climbed into my tiny, too-springy bottom bunk, lying side by side and still fully clothed. He moved his hand up my legs, from my knee to my inner thigh. There was no kissing, no lips pressed this place or that. But it was gentle. Nice.

We shifted a bit so my back pressed against his torso. It didn't occur to me to think about whether he was hard or not as his hand kept skimming the length of my leg. There was nothing weird between us, nothing cold or contrived. It felt good and I felt good.

But there was also nothing more that I wanted.

Nothing in me craved his hands to do more, explore further, despite enjoying every second of being close to him. He didn't force more on me, either. I didn't anticipate how secure I would feel in my body and in this place.

We were so comfortable, we fell asleep together with our clothes on.

When we woke up, we didn't continue what never really started, and it wasn't disappointing. That time together was satisfying and intimate. We lay together for a while, talking, and he told me he respected me—and my still being a virgin—too much to have sex with me just because he could. That was why he didn't push me to do more than what we did. His first time was memorable and with a girl he'd never forget. He said I should have the same with my first partner.

That conversation didn't change my perception of my virginity but it did change my perception of my worth when it came to having sex. I didn't need to accept any offer that came my way. I deserved to choose the exact right partner for me—or not to make the choice at all. I was worth that.

My group of friends still talked sex, about the nights they went home to see their boyfriends or girlfriends and got to finally release the tension they'd built in each other's absence. Or they talked about where on campus they'd had sex and where they'd love to have sex before graduation. The boy I didn't have sex with said before graduation he wanted to have sex in the college president's house (a task I'd help him pull off senior year).

But I didn't worry about my own sex life. There wasn't anyone in my immediate world who interested me romantically, let alone sexually. I could take care of myself as needed.

And then spring rolled around.

My friend—the boy I knew online but still hadn't met—debated with me over the course of that year about where he wanted to attend college. He'd come to like the school I was at and decided he wanted to visit campus. Not only was this a chance to see if the school fit, it was a chance for us to meet and see if we fit, too. Pressure without pressure.

As his visit drew closer, I told my group of friends about him, how we'd met in a writing forum and started talking years ago, how we'd never actually met. They asked what we planned to do when he got here, if he'd be spending the night with me. I was sincere when I said he'd do all of the routine campus visit things: go to a class, stay with a host student, eat in the cafeteria. I thought it would be fun if I could steal him for a few hours and have some time alone together in person for the first time. He and I had talked about sex plenty of times before, but it wasn't on my radar as something we'd actually *do* when we met for the first time.

The night he arrived, he dropped off his bags with his host and came to my room. I'd been nervous and excited, anxiously standing at my door looking out the peep hole, waiting to see his face for the first time in the flesh. There was no part of me worried he wouldn't be exactly who I'd gotten to know for four years. We'd exchanged photos and letters many times. I knew him almost as well as I knew myself.

But the first moment seeing him, having him in my room and in my space, was a surprise. He was full and present and more than I'd expected. When we hugged, he smelled good and felt better, softer even, than I imagined.

When we settled into the desk chairs in my room, he told me he had no plans for his night. Since there was a concert happening in the commons, we decided to go.

He and I exchanged glances and smiles, sitting close enough that our legs kept touching, setting off more glances, smiles. Excitement pulsed through my bones. I don't remember for the life of me who gave the concert. We stuck around until the end, bumping into more than a couple of my friends and making conversation that never once felt awkward or stilted, then headed toward my dorm.

It was a gorgeous, star-filled night. Rather than go inside to my room, I grabbed his hand and took him to my favorite spot: the bridge over the train tracks.

We had the place to ourselves. We walked to the middle of the bridge and stood side-by-side looking down at the tracks on the ground below. I told him how it felt to lie on my back when the train went by, how I could feel the wood planks rattle beneath me. About how when I needed to be alone, there was nowhere quieter than here.

The next train approached from the distance. We lay down and held hands as it barreled beneath us, laughing hard at the way the shaking bridge was terrifying and ticklish at the same time.

When we stopped to catch our breath from giggling, we leaned into one another and kissed.

We walked back to my dorm, electricity between our clasped hands. He wasn't going back to his host's room. My roommate was asleep in her top bunk, and the boy and I crawled into my bottom bunk. We kissed some more, kisses that were soft and hard, delicious and messy, before saying goodnight, both of us still in our clothes from the day. I'd shared a bed with other people before— guys and girls—but sharing it with him, especially after that kiss, was exciting.

I set the alarm so he could get up for the class he was visiting in the morning. But things didn't happen that way.

My roommate got up early and left, waking us before the alarm. After the door shut behind her, we lay facing each other, quiet. In that moment I knew, and so did he.

There was a spark.

The jar of condoms I'd been keeping sat inside my closet, and I grabbed the whole thing. Within minutes, his shirt and jeans were off, my shirt and shorts, too. He fumbled taking my bra off—the clasps a challenge for a rookie—and we lay chest to chest. The air was thick and warm, sweet and still. My skin flushed. Tingled.

I made the first move, grabbing a condom and handing it to him. He took off his boxers and rolled it on, while I slipped off my underwear. He was a virgin, too, which I knew from years of talking to one another. It was amazing how secure I felt with him, how being naked was the last thing on my mind. He wasn't judging me or analyzing the way I looked—and neither was I. My body wasn't in the way of the experience; my body was an important and worthy part of it.

We lay down and he slid inside me slowly. He was careful not to push too hard, asking if I was okay. Was he hurting me? Was this uncomfortable? Did he need to stop? Could he go a little harder or faster?

I was okay—better than okay. I didn't need him to stop because it felt good. I was relaxed, ready enough that he could move faster if he wanted to. Nothing was uncomfortable, though it was weird to have another person's body inside of my own. It was strange, but nice—really nice—to have his hands and mouth on my breasts. The insecurity I had about myself and my flaws didn't matter; he made me feel perfect the way I was. I experienced pleasure, all softness and tenderness and lightness, and I let myself have it.

While he pushed in and out of me, I became less aware of the physical act and more conscious of everything else: how calm my mind and emotions were, how right making this choice felt, how funny it was the bedsprings were so loud and that I hoped no one in the hall could hear. Maybe I didn't care if they did.

After he came, we triple-checked the condom to make sure it hadn't broken. I hadn't orgasmed, and he turned to using his fingers and his tongue to explore spaces of me I'd never shared with anyone else. There was no shame or vulnerability; it was exciting to be in this moment with him, to give and to take. When he'd tried for a while but wasn't successful at making me come, I told him it was fine if we crawled back under the covers and held each other. I felt good physically and emotionally.

The alarm went off a little while later and after another kiss, he went back to his host's room to change and get started on the rest of his college visit.

I skipped my class that day and settled into one of the seating areas in the commons, not far from where he and I had seen the concert the night before. I didn't want to be completely alone, and the quiet buzz of people going about their own business gave me the opportunity to sit with what happened. Was I different now? How would not being a virgin change me? Would it change me at all?

My thoughts returned to the afternoon in my room when my friend told me he respected me too much to sleep with me. I got to make the choice where and how I lost my virginity and I didn't have to accept an offer just to get it over with or because I claimed that it really didn't matter to me.

In that moment, I realized the autonomy I'd granted myself. I chose not to have sex with a friend in exchange for something silly like doing well on a test, even though I was comfortable with the idea. I chose to wait for the boy who I'd known and cared about for a long time.

The *where* and the *when* and the *how* didn't empower me, making the choice for myself did.

Beyond the Stories

It's Your Sex Life–Take Charge of It

If you've come this far, then you've got a pretty broad picture of what sex can be like—hot, meaningful, cringe-worthy, gross, forgettable, magnificent, empowering, transformative. There's a reason so many of us spend a lot of time thinking about and dreaming of sex. It is powerful—not to be taken lightly but maybe not necessarily taken too seriously either.

You get to express your sexuality in the way that's right for you. So take charge. Be the boss of your sexual self. Be the woman you want to be.

If that seems daunting, that's okay. I've got your back. The next section is jam-packed with resources. I interviewed four expert sex educators—Al Vernacchio, Pepper Schwartz, Jo Langford, and Amy Lang—and asked them to share what they've learned after years of working with young people. Consider this part of the book a map you can use to chart your own course through the steamy waters of sex.

Know Your Body

All the Parts
Start with the body.

All those curves and folds and slickery bits are worthy of your attention. Labia, mons pubis, vagina, clitoris—this is the territory of pleasure, and it's good to know your way around. Lots of women have never really looked at all their sexual parts. Sure it's hard to see down there, but the bigger issue is that many of us have the idea that looking is off limits.

But if you have plans to invite someone else into your nether regions, you should be able to get up close and personal with your own lady bits. Spending quality time with your body is a good precursor to sharing it with anyone else. If you need a diagram to find your way, there's a good one in *S-E-X: The All-You-Need-To-Know Progressive Sexuality Guide to Get You through High School and College* by Heather Corinna.

Use a mirror. Use your fingers. Explore.

Consider it information gathering, critical for sexual success.

Is That Normal?

Many of us wonder whether we look normal. Are my labia too long? Too dark? Are vaginas supposed to look like *that*? What about all my pubic hair? These concerns about the appearance of our sexual parts are exacerbated by the pervasiveness of pornography. Images of shaved, oiled, and surgically altered women are everywhere. Just as runway models don't reflect what the majority of women look like, neither do women in pornography.

Real women—and their sexual anatomy—come in all colors, shapes, and sizes. If you're worried that things look weird down there, check out the books *Body Drama: Real Girls, Real Bodies, Real Issues, Real Answers* by Nancy Redd, *Femalia* by Joani Blank, and *I'll Show You Mine* by Wrenna Robertson. These books feature full-color photographs of many different vaginas. Yours will fit right in.

Popping the Cherry

Sex educator Al Vernacchio says, "Misconceptions [about sex] are borne of misinformation or lack of information."[2] This confusion often starts with a maligned little bit of flesh called the hymen. The story goes that girls are born with a membrane covering the vaginal opening. First-time penis–in–vagina sex (penetrative sex) is supposed to hurt because an erection is bashing its way through this barrier. Blood on the sheets means the deal's been done. Proving virginity is as easy as prodding around up there to make sure the blockade is intact.

Except it doesn't work like this.

Like all parts of the female anatomy, there is a lot of variation from hymen to hymen. In some women this thin bit of tissue covers almost all of the vaginal opening. (It certainly doesn't cover the whole thing or we couldn't have periods.) Using a tampon or inserting a finger may stretch the tissue and cause discomfort. Other women may find no evidence of a hymen at all.

Like all the tissues down there, the hymen responds to arousal by becoming slick and elastic as you get turned on. Amy Lang says, "If everything is *all systems go*, [first-time sex] will feel good, not overwhelmingly painful."[3]

For a visual demo (and a lot more great info about sex) check out Laci Green's "You Can't POP Your Cherry" vlog post on her YouTube channel, *Sex+* (www.youtube.com/user/lacigreen).

Biological Sex vs. Gender

Biological sex is determined by sexual anatomy. Genetic makeup in tandem with conditions during fetal development influence how our genitals appear. A person can have a typically female reproductive system or a typically male reproductive system. When a combination of male, female, or ambiguous characteristics is present, the person is called intersex.

Gender is a whole different concept. Gender is how we identify ourselves. This is the core of who we are and is influenced by our intellectual and emotional selves as well as by cultural gender norms and expectations. Gender identity can occur on a spectrum, not just *woman* or *man*. People who identify on a part of the gender continuum that lies between woman and man often call themselves *genderqueer*.

Gender dysphoria occurs when biological sex and gender identity are not congruent. Sometimes this feeling is subtle or occasional, characterized by the impression that you differ from feminine norms. Other times there is a deep mismatch between the physical body and gender identity—a state of being called *transgender*. The word *cisgender* describes a match between sexual anatomy and gender identity.

For a wonderful discussion of the diverse manifestations of gender identity, check out these resources:

- *S-E-X: The All-You-Need-To-Know Progressive Sexuality Guide to Get You through High School and College* by Heather Corinna

- *Beyond Magenta: Transgender Teens Speak Out* by Susan Kuklin (a collection of personal essays)

- *Trans Bodies, Trans Selves: A Resource for the Transgender Community* by Laura Erickson-Schroth

- *Trans Lifeline* (www.translifeline.org, a nonprofit dedicated to transgendered people's well-being)

Know What Turns You On

Sexual Orientation—Don't Get Lost in the Letters

Many of us identify as *straight*, *gay*, or *lesbian*, but describing patterns of sexual attraction is not always as straightforward as it seems. *Bisexual* describes when a person feels sexual attraction for both men and women. Some prefer to identify as *queer, pansexual,* or *omnisexual* instead of bisexual because these terms acknowledge that gender and attraction occur on a spectrum. Those who find that sexual attraction isn't a big part of their lives sometimes identify as *asexual.*

What these terms fail to capture is the way our patterns of sexual attraction can change. They ebb and flow. Many people identify as *questioning* because they are engaged in an ongoing process of exploring their sexual orientation. You don't have to pick a label and stick with it.

Just as being familiar with your physical body is a prerequisite for initiating a sexual relationship, so is exploring your own patterns of sexual attraction. A good place to go for more information is Youth Resource, a website by and for lesbian, gay, bisexual, transgender, and questioning young people (www.youthresource.org). The book *GLBTQ: The Survival Guide for Gay, Lesbian, Bisexual, Transgender, and Questioning Teens* by Kelly Huegel is also a great resource.

Get Your Sexy On

Sex is as much mental as physical, and this is true for both women and men. You have probably heard a lot of generalizations about what turns men on (porn) versus what turns women on (romance), but like so much talk about sex, this glosses over the wide variety of real experiences.

Sexual arousal can be triggered by images, smells, or the lightest touch. Women like all kinds of sex and get turned on by all kinds of things. Maybe you like lingerie. Or maybe you're more of a flannel pajamas kind of gal. Sexual fantasies can be about people we know in real life, celebrities, or fictional characters. Sometimes we get turned on by imagining certain kinds of sex or sex in unusual locations.

It's important to remember that sexual fantasies are exactly that— fantasies. The thoughts that turn us on are not necessarily things we want to do in real life. A lot of women feel guilty about their fantasies. You don't need to. They're an important—and safe—way to explore your sexual needs and desires before you are involved with a partner.

Teasing the Kitty

Guys talk about masturbating a lot. They tell jokes. They brag about it. Mostly they feel comfortable with it. Jerking off is a way to feel good, release tension, and relax. There are tons of slang terms for male masturbation. *Spanking the monkey. Waxing the dolphin. Rubbing one out.* And it's pretty much culturally accepted that guys will do it.

As with most things sexual, there's a double standard for women. We rarely talk about female masturbation, and it is viewed more suspiciously than the same behavior in guys. Many girls begin masturbating when very young and worry that they're weird, but both girls and women can have a lot of fun *teasing the kitty* or *clicking the mouse.* It's totally normal and a completely safe way to explore what turns you on.

When and if you decide to engage in partnered sex, the person you are with won't automatically know what you need to be satisfied, but if *you* do, you can lead the way. As Jo Langford says, "A healthy experience is dependent on your relationship with yourself. Do you know how to make your own body feel good?"[4]

What about Orgasms?

They're nice. Very nice. Most people enjoy them. A lot.

Sometimes an orgasm is explosive—fireworks-style. Other times an orgasm is the peak of a long, slow, warm build. The experience will vary from person to person and from day to day. For most women, reaching orgasm involves direct stimulation to the clitoris. How to get yourself there is definitely something to explore during masturbation.

Orgasm can also be one of the real disconnects between partners during sex. Real life rarely looks like the romance novel
experience of mind-blowing, mutual (or multiple) climaxes. One
person coming first and deciding that's the end of sex can be deeply
unsatisfying for the other partner. Not all sexual encounters end
in orgasm, and that's okay, but healthy sexual partners are always
looking out for each other in bed.

Know What You're Up Against

Society Is a Sexual Minefield

Sex in the United States is a serious can of worms.

Al Vernacchio quotes a colleague who says that our society is
"sexually repressed to the point of being sexually obsessed."[5] On
the one hand, sex is candles, whip cream, feathers, and fireworks.
On the other, it's sinful, shameful, and wrong.

All of these contradictions put a lot of pressure on women. There
are so many expectations about how we should look, who we
should love, how we should act, and what we should feel.

Coming into our own as sexual people forces us to wade through
the muck of gender stereotypes:

Guys always want sex. Women want love.
It's okay if guys do it. Good girls wait.
Bad girls swallow.
If you like sex, you're a slut.

We deserve better. We deserve the chance to define ourselves. If
you want to explore how cultural expectations of women influence
our ability to be the women we want to be, check out TheFBomb.
org, an online community created by and for young people who
care about women's rights, and also teen activist Jules Spector's
blog at www.teenfeminist.com.

Us versus Them

Too often sex, especially straight sex, is presented as a battle. A real Casanova might brag about his many conquests as if each person he's been intimate with is a skirmish from which he's emerged victorious. First base, second, stealing third—the baseball metaphor for sexual accomplishments treats sex as a conflict zone. Somebody is always trying to score. Somebody is going to slide into home, even if the other side is trying to stop them.

There will be a winner and there will be a loser.

Ugh. Maybe we should all grab armor and suit up.

Al Vernaccio suggests it would be far more useful (and more fun) to think of sex like ordering pizza.[6] You do it when you're hungry, when you want to. Since you're sharing the meal with someone else, the two of you can talk about what toppings you want to order and when you want to eat. You discuss what you like, and then you sit at the table together with your pizza-eating sweetheart and enjoy yourselves. You don't even have to finish the meal to have a great time.

Whether you're craving pepperoni or mushroom and onion, it's a good idea to take sex out of the battlefield and into the realm of mutual satisfaction.

Porn Is Everywhere

We can't really talk about sex without talking about porn. Many an innocent Google search has led to hardcore sites. In a recent survey, eighteen-year-olds were asked at what age most young people started regularly viewing pornography. The most common answer was thirteen or fourteen.[7]

Because comprehensive, high-quality sex education is so rare in this country, many young people, especially boys, turn to porn as a primary source of information about sex. Every sex educator that I interviewed said many misconceptions arise from watching the highly artificial sex typically depicted in porn.

On every level, pornography is fantasy not reality.

Real women's bodies do not look like that. Make-up, body hair removal, professional set lighting, air-brushing and surgical enhancement to breasts, thighs, and even labia create porn star perfection. Real men's bodies don't look like that either—six-pack abs, shaved balls, and twelve-inch penises that stay hard forever are the result of manscaping and Viagra.

Al Vernacchio says, "What we see [in pornography] are fabricated situations that bear little to no resemblance to reality. Basing one's expectations about sex on what the media portrays is the best way to wind up with a lot of misconceptions."[8]

Real sex is very different from porn sex.

Porn makes it look like "sex starts with parts in holes," says Amy Lang.[9] Porn strips away the relationships and communication that are involved in real sex. Pepper Schwartz says that boys often think "they don't have to talk about anything,"[10] or they think, according to Jo Langford, "that real-life girls like being talked to the way porn girls are talked to"[11] and that "real-life girls want to be asked to do the same things."[12]

Young people often turn to porn to "learn how to *do sex*," says Jo Langford.[13] "Girls think they have to be a wild woman in bed to be sexy, and boys think they have to thrust like crazy and go as long as possible," adds Pepper Schwartz.[14] Boys learn that "they should be the aggressor when it comes to sex and they are surprised when girls are just as interested and push for it," adds Amy Lang.[15]

It turns out no one is learning much about real sex from pornography.

The Black Hole of Sex Ed

Pornography is not the place to learn about real sex but you can't count on sex education in schools either. There was a time (way back in the 1970s) when many public schools taught sex-positive, comprehensive sex education. Teens got complete and nonjudgmental information about their bodies, birth control, disease prevention, and healthy relationships. More revolutionary was the acknowledgment that sex and pleasure were interconnected.

Everything changed in the 1980s and 1990s.

New politics. New message. *Abstinence, abstinence, abstinence.* No sex before marriage.

A school sex ed film called *No Second Chances* shows a teen asking a nurse, "What if I want to have sex before I get married?"

Her answer?

"You'll just have to be prepared to die."[16]

What?!

That's right. Have sex and die.

The state of sex education in the United States has not improved since the 1990s. There are no national standards for content like there are for math or science. The Guttmacher Institute reports that in 2015 only twenty-two states require sex education at all, and only thirteen require that the information be accurate. Nineteen states teach abstinence but not contraception. Four states forbid teaching anything positive about nonheterosexual sex in schools.

So—

If you can't count on school for the information you need and pornography is make-believe, what are you supposed to do?

Know about Keeping It Safe

Get the Info

Taking charge of your sexual life means educating yourself about sex. It really is up to you. Seek out information from trusted sources. Websites like Scarleteen (www.scarleteen.com), Advocates for Youth (www.advocatesforyouth.org), and Sex, Etc. (sexetc.org) are a great place to start. On these sites, you can ask questions and read articles about everything from vibrators to oral sex to pregnancy. You can also find other resources that you might need. There are plenty of smart, fun books about sex that you can get from your local public library in many areas. Check the resource list at the end of this book for titles. You also might want to check out a series of online essays by teens about sex called "Teen Sex: It's Complicated" on the Huffington Post website (www.huffingtonpost.com).

On Safer Sex

This book is based on the belief that sex can and should be a positive, fulfilling, and deeply pleasurable part of our lives. That's not to say it is without risk. The *safer sex* approach to sexual activity may seem like a buzzkill, but nothing says *good-bye romance* like an unwanted pregnancy or a sexually transmitted infection.

To get the information you need to be prepared for healthy, safer sex, try places like your medical doctor or school-based health clinic. Several great resources include the article "Safe, Sound & Sexy: A Safer Sex How-To" on the Scarleteen website, Planned Parenthood (www.plannedparenthood.com), Bedsider (bedsider.org), and *Sex: A Book for Teens* by Nikol Hasler.

The absolute basics are:

- Monitor your sexual health with regular gynecological exams and screening for sexually transmitted infections (STIs), also referred to as sexually transmitted diseases (STDs). This should happen at least once a year and more often if you have multiple partners. Your partners need to get tested too.

- Get vaccinated against human papillomavirus (HPV). This common STI is spread through vaginal, anal, and oral sex, and often has no symptoms. Having HPV greatly increases your risk of cervical cancer. The vaccine, which is given to both men and women, is easy, permanent protection.

- Use barriers like condoms, dental dams, and latex gloves to protect from infection. Don't wait until you're sweaty and naked to figure out how to use these things. Grab a girlfriend and go buy various kinds of condoms. Check them out. Slide them on a banana. If you bring the condoms, it does not mean you are a slut. It means you value yourself enough to be safe and prepared.

- If there is a penis involved in your sexual activities, reliable birth control, such as the pill, hormone shots, implants, or cervical rings, is essential. And remember, nonbarrier methods won't protect against STIs so you still need that condom with spermicide. Every. Single. Time. If the penis-owner complains then he should take his unclad cock and play with it himself.

- Consider and reconsider the kinds of sexual activity that you plan to engage in. Some are much more risky than others. Any kind of unprotected sex, even oral sex, is riskier than protected sex. Check out the risk assessment list in *S-E-X: The All-You-Need-To-Know Progressive Sexuality Guide to Get You through High School and College* by Heather Corinna.

The Age of Consent

When I asked Jo Langford what advice he had for young people thinking about becoming sexually active, he said, "Do due diligence to avoid knowingly or accidentally doing something that could harm someone (including yourself)."[17]

It's really important that you know the age of potential sexual partners. Age differences often mean power differences. Who can drive? Who can't? Is one person old enough to buy alcohol?

Age matters. It can even make sex illegal.

Every state has *age of consent* laws for sex, which is the age a person can legally agree to sex.

In the US, the age of consent varies from sixteen to eighteen depending on the state. Some (but not all) states have an age-gap provision, meaning that two fifteen-year-olds could have sex without risk of prosecution. You should know what the law is in your state. In many places, if a fifteen-year-old and an eighteen-year-old have sex, the older person could be charged with rape even if the younger person was a willing participant.

Sexual Assault

The prevalence of sexual assault, including rape, in the United States is staggering. Almost one out of every six women has been the victim of a sexual crime.[18] Teenagers from ages sixteen to nineteen are four times more likely to be victims of sexual assault than any other segment of the population.[19] One in five college women has been sexually victimized while at college,[20] and the vast majority of these assaults are committed by men known to the victim.[21]

We live in a culture that struggles to support victims of sexual crimes. Only 32 percent of sexual assaults are reported to the police.[22] Ninety-seven percent of rapists will never go to jail.[23] Too often, a woman reporting a rape is the one blamed for inciting the assault. *She was drunk. She dressed like a slut. She asked for it.*

Conversations about rape in our culture tend to be about ways in which women can protect themselves from being raped. This implies that if we just do the right things, we will always be safe. The statistics tell us that this simply isn't true.

Responsibility for rape lies with the perpetrator. Rape is never the fault of the victim. Unwanted sex is unwanted even if the victim didn't scream *no* at the top of her lungs, even if she was into making out and then wanted to stop, even if she was drunk when it happened.

If you are assaulted, it's not your fault, you didn't deserve it, and there are people who want to help you. Most cities have rape crisis centers. The organization RAINN can locate the one nearest you (centers.rainn.org). The National Sexual Assault Telephone Hotline can be reached at 1-800-656-HOPE (4673).

Safer Sex, Recreational Drugs, and Alcohol

One of the reasons people like to drink, especially in social situations, is that it loosens us up. With a few drinks on board, we don't worry so much. We get rowdy. We take more risks. That's probably okay if you're trying to get your nerve up to do karaoke, but in sexually charged situations being drunk makes it harder to establish boundaries. Many of us have found ourselves, hungover as hell, in beds we wish we hadn't woken up in. With our beer goggles on, we weren't so picky about who we got naked with. Maybe we were too drunk to bother with a condom. Maybe that was our best friend's girlfriend.

It happens.

But it's not the route to safer sex.

If you know that you'll be heading into a high-risk party situation, set up a buddy system with a friend so you can support each other. In general, if you limit the booze, you'll be in a far better position to advocate for yourself and what you want.

A Picture Is Worth a Thousand Words

There's probably a cell phone in your pocket. It's probably a smart phone with a camera and access to the internet. With a few clicks you can answer almost any question. Friends are a text away. The downside to having the world at your fingertips is that the world can get up in your business faster than you can blink.

And trust me, there are places you don't want the fingers of the world.

Sending a sexy picture of yourself might feel like no big deal. It's fun and a little naughty to doll up and try out a porn star pose. Maybe your boyfriend asks for a picture of your breasts to get him through the next twenty-four hours without you. Maybe your girlfriend wants to see you touch yourself.

A sexy picture between two people who trust each other shouldn't really be a big deal, but sexts (or any kind of sexually explicit texts, emails, instant messages, online posts, or chats) can turn around to bite you on the ass. Everyone seems to be doing it, from movie stars to the straight-A student who sits next to you in calculus. In a recent survey, 46 percent of teenagers agree that "sending sexual or naked photos or videos is part of everyday life for teenagers nowadays,"[32] but sexting can have consequences you never even considered.

Break up with your sweetie and you might find that those private pictures have a whole new life. With a single click, a picture can be sent to everyone you know—friends, teachers, parents. There are accounts on social media sites like Instagram and Tumblr that aggregate and share naked pictures. Best-case scenario, it's embarrassing. Worst-case scenario, it's a crime. Depending on the state you live in, sending naked pictures, even of yourself, can be prosecuted under child pornography laws. Sexual pictures have been used to blackmail young women for sex, to humiliate them in public, and even to encourage sex offenders to go to their houses.

The internet never forgets either. Long after you send them, sexts can return to haunt you. Most hiring managers do an internet search on job applicants. A close-up of your cleavage might not be the first thing you want them to see. College coaches routinely check social media before recruiting teen athletes. You don't want to lose out on a scholarship because you took off your pants.

So at the risk of sounding like a nag—*no pictures, no pictures, no pictures.*

Not of you.

Not of your partner.

Not of anyone's sexy bits.

Have all the fun you want, but make memories, not evidence.

Know How to Talk About It

Pick Your Words

Vagina, pussy, vajayjay, hooty-hoo.
Breasts, tatas, tits, boobs.
Penis, cock, boner, dick.
Intercourse, screwing, making love, fucking.

Talking about sex means knowing and using real and accurate words and also finding the words you feel comfortable using. Trust me, there are plenty to choose from. (Check out the historical *Timeline of Slang Terms for the Vagina* compiled by Jonathon Green.) You've got to have words to talk the talk. And I don't mean The Talk. I mean real conversations about sex with friends, parents, and partners. At first this is going to be awkward as all get-out—blushing, sweaty pits, giggles, the whole shebang—especially with parents, but as Al Vernacchio says, "Healthy sexual activity has to be deliberate, communicative, and honest."[24]

What about Talking to Parents?

The truth is your parents are as nervous about these conversations as you are.

Amy Lang says, "Most parents do not want to even think about their kids having sex, so when a teen is brave and smart enough to bring it up, they need to be ready for some parental freak-out. It's a really good idea to plan what you want to say before you say it and be ready for their responses."[25]

Pepper Schwartz advises starting the conversation way before you're in the middle of a hot and heavy relationship. You could say that you know you will eventually get serious about someone and there will probably be times you want to be sexual. Tell your parents that you don't know enough to be safe about it and don't want to be sorry about what happens. Ask for their advice and values around sex even if you end up choosing a different path.[26]

Jo Langford suggests asking specific questions. "Parents are often reluctant about sharing their personal stories because they don't want to say too much, freak you out, or make you think differently of them. Questions such as, 'What was your first sexual experience like?' give them permission to speak freely."[27]

Check out the book *100 Questions You'd Never Ask Your Parents* by Elisabeth Henderson and Nancy Armstrong, MD, and consider asking your parents some of these questions.

Nobody likes a high-pressure situation, so asking questions as they come up in casual conversation—maybe a scene in a movie sparks a discussion about consent, for example—takes the heat off of everyone. The more you engage with your parents about sex-based topics, the easier and more natural the conversations become. It's always better to talk before there's a problem.

If you feel absolutely sure that you cannot go to your parents with questions about sex, seek out another trustworthy adult, perhaps an older sibling, an aunt, or a medical provider. Amy Lang points out that "You have a right to see your doctor alone. Make up an excuse and go."[28] Your sexual health is an important part of your overall health.

What about Talking to Your Partner?

The other person you need to be talking sex with is definitely your partner.

- How experienced is each of you?

- What sexual activities do you want to try?

- What's your birth control plan?

- What about preventing STIs?

- What does sex mean in the context of your relationship—a hookup, friends-with-benefits, a commitment to an ongoing relationship?

According to Al Vernacchio, "Every sexual encounter starts with two unique individuals who are creating an entirely new experience. Healthy sexual interactions begin with each of us being our authentic selves. We're not playing a role, putting on a mask, or trying to be someone else. When we're honest about what we want and don't want, when we feel good about our decisions, and when we know why we're doing what we do, those are some of the ingredients for successful sexual encounters."[29]

And he adds, "If you can't look your partner in the eye and talk about what you want to do, then you aren't ready to do it."[30]

Solidifying Your Values

Feeling good is great, except when it's so good that we get swept away. And that happens. We're in the moment. There's kissing and licking, and those hands on your breasts feel amazing. Clothes end up on the floor, and you're really wet. There's all this desire and need and stopping sounds terrible and there's no condom, but it feels so good . . . .

Boundaries—you've got to know what yours are.

How far do you want to go? Where do you want to stop? And why?

Decisions about sexual intimacy should be based on what you value. Ask yourself how sex fits into your respect for yourself, your plans for the future, your sense of what sex means to you, and your relationship with a partner.

Amy Lang says, "The absolute best way to navigate [peer pressure to have sex] is to be really, super clear about your sexual values. This means understanding how far you are willing to go and under what circumstances. It means being clear about what you want your first time to be like."[31]

Her book *Dating Smarts: What Every Teen Needs to Know to Date, Relate, or Wait* is a good place to explore your values around sex. Knowing your boundaries will give you strength to slow down or stop if going all the way is not part of your plan, even when it feels great.

Know When You're Ready

Everyone's Doing it, Aren't They?

Ever notice how sometimes it seems like there is a sex superhighway? Everyone is on it, driving a hundred miles an hour. Merging is a bitch. You've got to hope you don't crash. Everyone is rush, rush, rushing to get there—wherever *there* is. No one wants to be the last virgin in the room.

Slow down. Hit the brakes. Let's throw some facts at this racetrack.

Here are the current stats about sexual activity in young people: 16 percent of fifteen-year-olds, 33 percent of sixteen-year-olds, 48 percent of seventeen-year-olds, and 61 percent of eighteen-year-olds have had sex. The numbers are pretty much the same for young women and men. The average age of first-time sex is seventeen.[33]

The first times described in this book cover a huge range. The youngest was thirteen. The oldest twenty-three. It's pretty clear that just because everyone seems to be bragging about sex it doesn't mean they've actually had it.

Being Ready

Let's forget the *go, go, go* for a minute and focus on figuring out when *you* are ready to take on sex.

With real driving there's a program: take the written test, drive with a learner's permit, maybe take driver's ed. Eventually you spend an excruciating morning at the Department of Motor Vehicles and then—boom!—you're qualified. It's not so easy with sex. After all, you're facing this big unknown experience. It's hard to know if you're ready for something mysterious that you've never done.

Jo Langford says, "A person is ready for sex when their brain, their heart, and their crotch all come online and are functioning at the same general level. But hearts and crotches fire up for many people before the brain can catch up, and that can lead to poor decisions and unfortunate consequences. For some people this combo of drive, emotional readiness, and logic-plus-education doesn't happen until their twenties. It's the rare person who has all of this going on before sixteen."[34]

Amy Lang's perspective is similar. For her, being ready means being able to "wholeheartedly say yes to everything. Yes to open communication. Yes to being on birth control. Yes to condoms. Yes to getting STI testing. Yes to this particular partner. Yes to understanding what sex means to the relationship. Yes to having a safe place to do it. Yes to knowing this is the right person, time, and place."[35]

In the Moment

This is it.

You're hot.

You're ready.

This person next to you is the one.

It's time to get swept away in the moment but not the time to get sucked into doing things you don't want to do.

Sexual agency—the power to choose what we want to do sexually—is imperative. There is no time during a sexual encounter where you have gone too far to say *I want to stop*. You don't have to do anything you don't want to do, and neither does your partner.

Consent sounds like—

Can I kiss you? Yes!

Is it okay if I touch you there? Yes!

Do you want me to do this? Yes!

It's not the dialogue from a porn script. It's not the sultry pillow talk of romance novels. But jubilant consent is sexy.

As we said at the beginning, the real V-word—the most important one—is *VOICE*. Saying *yes*, saying *no*, saying *I'm not sure*—using your voice is an essential part of having feel-good, thrilling sexual experiences.

Now—

In the moment—

With protection, intention, and *yes*, you can enjoy being closer than close to another person. It's a big deal, especially the first time. Take it seriously. Be kind. Give and receive.

And have fun.

The Power of Story

A Conversation between
Kelly Jensen and Amber Keyser

The women who wrote the essays in this book did so because words are powerful. The way we talk about our bodies and our sexual experiences matters. When we tell our stories, we shape the lives we are actually living. We offer them to you in the hopes that these stories will illuminate the range of possible sexual experiences. Sometimes stories are mirrors held up to our own experience.

Our stories illuminate the universals. We want to love and be loved. We want to belong. We want to find our own path amid the expectations of friends, family, religion, and culture. We want to be the heroes in our own lives.

When it comes to sex and all the wonderful, complicated ways it intersects with the rest of our lives, more stories can only be a good thing. This chapter is a conversation between me and Kelly Jensen, a teen media specialist, about depictions of sex in media, particularly in young adult novels. We hope it will give you some good ideas about where to look to find the mirrors and windows you need to take charge of your own sexual life.

AMBER: Conversations about sex can be hard because of language. We know words matter, especially sex words. They can be clinical or nasty or euphemistic. How does media directed toward teens reflect the language we use to talk about sex and sexual experiences?

KELLY: It's not very good.

Our experiences can only be filtered through our words, so when our language is euphemistic or clinical, we can't describe the female sexual experience in an authentic way. Vagina and clitoris describe physical parts, but they're not words that roll easily off the tongue. The vast majority of slang terms for the female anatomy are insulting in one way or another. They're words that describe anatomy rather than experiences or feelings relating to sex and sexual experiences.

It's easier to describe what happens when a boy is turned on. We say *he gets hard*, and everyone knows what that means, what it looks like, and how it feels. It's not clinical or derogatory. It's an action. For girls an entire range of physical reactions can happen during arousal but we very rarely read descriptions of the process.

Author E. M. Kokie wrote a great blog post called "In Our Own Words" (http://emkokie.com/attractive_nuisance/2013/05/09/in-our -own-words) about the lack of language to describe female sexual experiences compared to male sexual experiences. One thing she notes is that romantic and intimate scenes often fade to black. Readers don't hear a female character talking about what's happening to her body, how she's reacting to touch, what it feels like physically, or the changes she's experiencing. Maybe she's aware of it and maybe she's not, but it's just not there in most books for teens.

Lauren Myracle's *The Infinite Moment of Us* offers an honest and solid portrayal of female arousal. It's forthright but feels neither clinical nor nasty. The main character, Wren, describes how when she's turned on, her breathing changes, her nipples get hard, and she grows wet. More powerfully, though, Wren doesn't get embarrassed. She is excited about her body being her body and doing the things a body does when it's ready for pleasure.

AMBER: It seems like no one ever has a neutral conversation about sex. People have pretty strong feelings about the topic and tend to jump on the judgment bandwagon right away. How do labels like *slut* or *prude* influence the way we tell stories about sex?

KELLY: *Slut* and *prude* are value judgments used to keep a woman in line or put her in her place socially. A *slut* is easy and worthless, while a *prude* is uptight and naive. Labeling takes away sexual autonomy from women. There is a whole spectrum of sexual experiences that we can choose to engage in or not. Labels give a false, limiting sense that a women's sexual choices make her good or bad—often called slut-shaming or prude-shaming.

One of the best examples of how and why these labels are damaging is explored in Mariko and Jillian Tamaki's *This One Summer*. Rose and her family hit the same beach every summer for vacation, where she is reunited with her younger friend Windy. This particular summer, Rose and Windy find themselves tuned in to the kids who live in the resort town year-round, and Rose starts referring to some of the girls as *sluts*. Windy calls her out on it, and Rose has to pause and reflect upon why she's using the language she is to describe girls she doesn't even know, what those judgments really mean, and what it might feel like were she at the receiving end of such labels.

In Jennifer Mathieu's *The Truth about Alice*, we see what happens when one girl's sexual reputation becomes the focal point for a tragedy that rocks the town. It's a tough look at how rotten people can be toward a girl when she is seen as little more than the town slut. Labeling Alice allows people to ignore and dehumanize her.

A small number of titles like *Pure* by Terra Elan McVoy and *Purity* by Jackson Pearce explore purity pledges, a growing movement in the United States in which a girl vows, often in the presence of her religious community, to remain a virgin. Hardly any books look at virginity as a personal choice made by a girl and what the social ramifications are for her.

In *Looking for Alibrandi* by Melina Marchetta, Josie decides she's not ready to have intercourse with her boyfriend, despite the fact she enjoys the touching and exploration going on with him. She tells Jacob that she's not ready. The place isn't right, the mood isn't right, and her virginity is something she wants to enjoy sharing with someone on her own terms. Jacob rebuffs her, suggesting she's being a prude about going further, but Josie tells him that making a choice about her body is something only she gets to do. He's upset at first, but eventually he realizes that he's the one being a jerk.

Diana Peterfreund's duology *Rampant* and *Ascendant* features girls who grapple with their choices about virginity as well.

The bottom line is that we need to be careful with language. Labels and the judgments they carry limit our ability to talk about what a sexually fulfilling and empowered life looks and feels like.

AMBER: I love watching *Modern Family*, *Orange Is the New Black*, *The Fosters*, and *Orphan Black*. It's awesome to see same-sex relationships and transgender issues depicted in such a normalizing way on television. Can you talk about depictions of sexual orientation, gender identity, and the shifting nature of sexuality?

KELLY: There is an increasing number of excellent books featuring LGBTQ characters and themes for young adult readers like *The Difference between You and Me* by Madeleine George, *The Miseducation of Cameron Post* by Emily M. Danforth, *Aristotle and Dante Discover the Secrets of the Universe* by Benjamin Alire Saenz, *Empress of the World* by Sara Ryan, *Two Boys Kissing* by David Levithan and *Openly Straight* by Bill Konigsberg.

But I want to go into more detail about titles that push the boundaries even further.

Far from You by Tess Sharpe features a bisexual main character, who actually uses the word bisexual to describe herself. This goes back to our conversation about the power of language. It's important and validating for readers to see precise descriptions of sexuality.

Nina LaCour's *Everything Leads to You* is a solid lesbian romance in which the main character, Emi, is a person of color. Another fantastic, racially diverse story is *Not Otherwise Specified* by Hannah Moskowitz. Bisexual main character Etta is open and positively *owns* her queerness.

In *Adaptation* and *Inheritance*, author Malinda Lo depicts a main character who can't choose between a boy and a girl. She's got feelings for both that she wants to pursue. In a great twist, Lo allows her main character to have both partners at once. It's a relationship to which they all consent and an arrangement which brings them all satisfaction. Alaya Dawn Johnson's *The Summer Prince* features bisexuality and polyamory in a nonwhite society.

I've got to mention Libba Bray's *Beauty Queens* here. Though it's a satire, Bray offers characters who explore and identify all along the sexuality spectrum in a way that's not just refreshing but reflects what our world looks like.

Notable transgender and transsexual stories include Kirstin Cronn-Mills's *Beautiful Music for Ugly Children* and Julie Anne Peters's *Luna*. The nonfiction work *Beyond Magenta: Transgender Teens Speak Out* by Susan Kuklin profiles transgender and gender-neutral teenagers, giving us an important look at real teens who are exploring their gender identities. Two additional nonfiction memoirs about gender reassignment to note include *Some Assembly Required* by Arin Andrews and *Rethinking Normal* by Katie Rain Hill.

For a non-Western story of sexuality, there's Sara Farizan's *If You Could Be Mine*, set in Iran. Farizan's novel is about two girls who are in love but legally can't be together, so one considers a sex change, a procedure legal in Iran, in order to be with the girl she loves.

Liz Prince's memoir *Tomboy* shows what it feels like to be pressured to conform to what society sees as acceptable gender appearances. Prince doesn't like dressing in a manner that girls are "supposed to," and must confront what it means to be true to herself.

Stories like these capture the reality of today's world. It's not all straight and white, male and female. It's a variety of colors, shapes, and desires. Sexuality is a spectrum, and gender identities are not set in stone.

AMBER: For women especially, how we feel about our bodies is a huge part of how we experience sex. That's a theme that came out in many of the essays in this book. How do you see the relationship between body image and sexuality intersecting in fiction?

KELLY: How often do we really talk honestly about body image? There's a Body Image and Eating Disorder Awareness Week, but we live in a world where "plus-size" models are size ten, and everything is photoshopped. We applaud underwear companies like Aerie that don't retouch models in their advertising and get emotional about Dove soap campaigns featuring women of varying shapes and sizes. But even these companies only showcase a tiny fraction of the range of body shapes, sizes, and features found in real women. That's weird, isn't it?

But back to sex and body image. Growing up I was told that I'd be ready to have sex when I could perform naked cartwheels in front of my partner. That would mean I was truly okay with my body and ready to share it with someone else. But that's silly and really demeaning.

Body image and sexuality are inextricably connected because sex is about our bodies. Even if it's not necessarily about how they look, it's about what they can do and the things they feel. Sex makes our bodies feel good, but it doesn't make our body image insecurities suddenly disappear. Many of us struggle with varying levels of body acceptance. That's okay. But there's also no doubt that being secure in your body can be an important part of sharing it with someone else.

One of the best novels that explores the relationship between body image and sex is Susan Vaught's *My Big Fat Manifesto*. Jamie acknowledges that her body is fat but she's comfortable in her own skin. Jamie pursues and enjoys sex, and the way her body looks has no bearing on what it does or how it can feel when she's enjoying herself. What makes this book even more special is that Jamie's boyfriend Burke decides he's not comfortable with his weight and chooses to get bypass surgery. Jamie recognizes that other people don't feel as comfortable with themselves as she does and that's okay too.

A nonfiction title worth looking at is Nancy Amanda Redd's *Body Drama*, which features color photographs of many different women naked, including close-ups of breasts and vaginas, as well as down-to-earth talk about body image.

AMBER: One of the common stereotypes about sex is that for women it's all emotional but for men it's one big physical explosion. What do you think? Any truth there or is that all bullshit?

KELLY: If that were the case, then girls would never be interested in hookups.

Girls have a wide range of responses to sex. For some, it's exceptionally emotional—it's totally normal to cry if you're having a good time. For others, it's entirely physical—your body can just feel amazing when you're having a good time.

Every single person is different and each sexual experience is different. Even regular sex with the same partner can be unique in every encounter: sometimes it's emotional, sometimes it's not, and, maybe most of the time, it falls between being very emotional and very physical.

In Daria Snadowsky's *Anatomy of a Single Girl*, Dominique struggles with the idea of having sex with a guy for the sake of having sex. She's just broken up with her first love, and the idea of hooking up with a guy for the fun of it seems beyond her. She's a "good girl." But the more she engages, the less scary sex for physical pleasure becomes. There's a scene where she pushes her partner down and straddles him, taking total control of intercourse. Being on top allows her to achieve sexual satisfaction in a way she never has before. This is a turning point for Dominique because she discovers how awesome her body is and how great it can feel.

The main character in *Biggest Flirts* by Jennifer Echols is not interested in commitment nor is she seeking emotional satisfaction. Tia wants a good time and nothing more. Her approach to sex is shame-free and empowering.

Sarah Dessen deserves recognition here, too, for offering readers a sexually active and empowered main character in *The Moon and More*. Emaline enjoys sex with her long-time boyfriend, Luke. It's a fun, healthy part of their relationship. When it's time for her to break it off with Luke, sex isn't a string keeping them together. It isn't the whole of her.

AMBER: Often a precursor to good sexual experiences is knowing your way around your own body, but it still seems like masturbation, especially when it comes to women, is hardly talked about. Where do we see positive depictions of female masturbation?

KELLY: There's an excellent piece in *Rookie: Yearbook One* (a compilation edited by Tavi Gevinson), about female masturbation that reminded me how important it is to have open conversations about solo sex. There is nothing more empowering than knowing your own geography.

In *The F— It List* by Julie Halpern, Becca, who has cancer, makes a bucket list for her best friend Alex to complete. One of the items is for Alex to masturbate. She feels more uncomfortable with the idea of masturbation than she does having sex with a partner. But Alex follows through on the list even though she feels guilty that she gets to masturbate while Becca's in chemotherapy. The open and honest conversations between Becca and Alex are empowering and validating, both to them and to readers.

In *Anatomy of a Boyfriend* by Daria Snadowsky, Dominique purposefully gets to know her own body before she engages in sexual activities with her boyfriend so she will have a better idea of what it's going to feel like. Other depictions of teen girls masturbating and enjoying it include Fiona Woods' *Wildlife*, Kody Keplinger's *The DUFF*, and Sarah McCarry's *All Our Pretty Songs*. Of course, Judy Blume was a pioneer here, too, with *Deenie*.

AMBER: I think we should talk about romance novels. I remember waiting on the hold list at the library for six months to get a copy of a bodice-ripper called *The Savage Sands*. It doesn't take many sexual experiences to realize that romance novels are not reality, but do they have something to offer in the all-about-sex conversation?

KELLY: Absolutely!

It's important to look at romances not as a roadmap to how the real world of sex works, but as stories that encourage women to take control of their romantic and sexual lives. It's so validating to see a heroine take the reins and go for what she wants. Romance is exciting—and sometimes even feels forbidden—because the focus is on female pleasure. Women in romance novels have great orgasms and get happy endings.

Romance novels also allow teens to enjoy some seriously hot sex in a way that works at their level of comfort. Too hot? Shut the book or skim the pages. Not hot enough? There are thousands of other titles to choose from. Even the act of being able to pick and choose what kind of spice you want to read is an exercise in control and comfort with sex.

The same can be said of erotic fan fiction. Lots of steamy, sexy material is written and consumed by young women. It's a safe outlet to explore what they like and what brings them satisfaction. That's powerful!

AMBER: Some of the most frequently challenged books are ones dealing with sexual violence like *The Bluest Eye* by Toni Morrison and *Speak* by Laurie Halse Anderson. Is this a topic we need to protect young people from reading about?

KELLY: Part of why those books are challenged and censored is that they make adults uncomfortable. Just as it is hard for most parents to discuss sex in a healthy, productive way with their teens, they don't want to talk about sexual violence either. But we have to talk about in order to have any hope of curtailing it.

It would be great if the real world were always safe and unproblematic but the truth is lots of hard, sad, terrible things happen to young people. Books reflect those experiences. Blocking readers from difficult content doesn't make them safer or more innocent. Fiction is a safe space to explore hard topics like sexual violence.

In addition to Anderson's groundbreaking and life-changing *Speak*, other titles continue to blaze trails. Christa Desir's *Fault Line*, told from the male point of view, delves into his girlfriend's experience being sexually violated and the fallout she endures when it's not clear what has happened to her. Brandy Colbert's *Pointe* features an adult of legal age pursuing and becoming intimate with an underage girl in a way that haunts her deeply for a long time.

Uses for Boys by Erica Lorraine Scheidt offers a story about a girl who has various sexual experiences, some good and some violent. *The Mockingbirds* by Daisy Whitney is about a girl who experiences sexual violence and pursues justice for herself, even though she knows it means she might not be seen in the most favorable light, if she's even listened to at all.

Other titles that tackle aspects of sexual violence worth mentioning include *One Lonely Degree* by C. K. Kelly Martin, *Tricks* by Ellen Hopkins, *Live through This* by Mindi Scott, *Faking Normal* by Courtney C. Stevens, and *Just Listen* by Sarah Dessen.

The bottom line is that we should put more faith in young people and their ability to tackle tough subjects in their reading material. Teens are amazing self-censors and know when they can't read something because they're uncomfortable with it or it's too much to handle. We need to talk with them about these stories. They deserve that.

AMBER: In 2012, a group of high school boys from Steubenville High School repeatedly raped one of their peers and posted the assault on social media. This horrific rape triggered a nationwide conversation about rape culture. Are there any good books that take on this difficult issue?

KELLY: Let's start with a definition: "rape culture" means a society where many practices and beliefs legitimize sexual violence and shift the focus from the violator to the victim.

Think about dress codes in school. The rules aimed at girls can go on for paragraphs—don't wear short skirts, low-cut tops, leggings, certain makeup, and so forth. Why? So you're not a "distraction." So boys can control themselves. Often rape victims are accused of wearing slutty clothes and therefore "asking for it." If a woman has had multiple sexual partners, then she obviously deserved to be raped.

We live in a world where women are constantly shamed and reminded that our very existence is a distraction to men. Discussions of rape focus almost exclusively on the things women can do to prevent rape instead of on raising boys into men who would never sexually assault another person.

The outcry after Steubenville wasn't about the victim and how her life was irrevocably changed. It was about the "poor boys" and how their futures were now tarnished. That's rape culture.

As for depictions in fiction, *All the Rage* by Courtney Summers is a must-read. It exposes some ugly truths about our social commitment to protecting boys and their actions at the expense of girls' bodies, emotional well-being, and futures. The story reveals what it is like to be a victim of rape and have an entire community turn against you. This book is a wake-up call about the importance of listening to and believing victims of sexual violence.

Patty Blount's *Some Boys* tackles some similar elements of rape culture, with the added perspective of what it's like to be a boy who is caught between believing what happened to a girl he likes and coming to terms with the fact his best friend may be the rapist.

AMBER: The opposite of rape is consent—ideally enthusiastic consent. Are there good examples in fiction of healthy ways young people talk about sex with potential partners?

KELLY: I'm glad we're seeing more focus in media for teens on consent and what that really means. A huge part of combating rape culture will be conversations with boys and men about the importance of asking whether they can do things with their partner—*Can I kiss you? Can I touch you there?* It's simple and nonnegotiable.

Part of the problem is how often sex is seen as just penetration, rather than a landscape of sexual behaviors. Intercourse is the *yes* or *no* point instead of the sexual experience as a whole being a series of steps and discussions.

Sarah Ockler's *Twenty Boy Summer* is a great example of sexual consent. Jolene Perry's *The Summer I Found You* is another solid example. There's an actual conversation between the couple, wherein it's laid out that when one person says *pause* or *stop*, then the activity does just that. The third book in Myra McEntire's Hourglass series, *Infinityglass*, features a boy who asks the girl if he has "a green light" to continue when they're getting into it. Dunn and Hallie build trust into their relationship through their conversation about whether what is happening is comfortable and okay.

There are more layers to consent, too, as is seen in A. S. King's *Ask the Passengers*. Astrid isn't ready to take her relationship with Dee as far as Dee wants to, and the message here is that not explicitly saying no isn't the same as being enthusiastic, consenting, and saying yes. In Leila Sales's *This Song Will Save Your Life*, there's a scene where Vicky witnesses a group of guys attempting to make out with a drunk girl. She approaches them, firmly stating that the girl is too drunk to consent, and rather than leave the drunk girl there or wait to hear pushback from the boys, Vicky takes the girl out of the situation.

Another great example of consent is in Katie Cotugno's *How to Love*. Sawyer asks Reena if she's ready for sex—twice—and waits for her solid *yes* before going further.

AMBER: One of the big ideas in this book is that young women can and should take charge of their sexuality, whether that means saying yes or saying no. Do you have any favorite examples of sexually empowered female characters?

KELLY: One of my favorite depictions of female sexuality is in the animated TV sitcom *Bob's Burgers*. Tina, the oldest daughter, always has sex on her mind in a way that's usually depicted with male characters. Her friends and family tease her about it but it's in good fun, rather than ridicule or degradation. They don't suggest that writing erotic fan fiction is going to kill her. They don't tell her that being in love with boys or butts or finding other people's sex lives fascinating is wrong. Instead, she can explore her own sexual desires in a safe space.

Trish Doller's *Where the Stars Still Shine* is one of the only books featuring a boy giving a girl oral sex. Main character Callie enjoys every single second of it without shame. She reclaims her own pleasure after experiencing sexual violence, showcasing that each person's healing process after victimization is unique. There's no set of standards, no rule book.

In *Sex & Violence* by Carrie Mesrobian, sexually empowered Baker is confident in herself. She teases Evan without being mean. It's a playful reminder that not all girls who like sex are easy.

Isla in Stephanie Perkins's *Isla and the Happily Ever After* is empowered, too. When she and Josh begin their relationship, he teases her about her experiences since she's quiet and shy. She isn't naive, and their relationship is physical from the beginning in a way she wants and enjoys immensely. That the bulk of their relationship is physical is something she desires.

Sara Zarr and Tara Altebrando's *Roomies* also depicts sexuality in a positive and empowering way. Both Elizabeth and Lauren are in relationships throughout the story. One of the girls loses her virginity, while the other doesn't, but there's no shaming of one girl from the other, and the sexual experience is realistically portrayed.

Amy Spalding's *Ink Is Thicker than Water* is one of the most honest depictions of sexual awkwardness—and autonomy—in young adult literature. Kellie had the opportunity to have sex with Oliver prior to the start of the novel and chose not to. Ever since, she's worried her chances of ever having a relationship with him again are gone. If she'd hurt him before by saying no, why would he want to pursue her? But Oliver does. As their relationship develops, Kellie constantly questions her readiness, but when she decides to have sex with him, she understands the role sex can play in their relationship and that she gets to make her own decision about it. What's especially great is that the sex is awkward and strange for Kellie to think and talk about, and it's awkward in the moment too. It's refreshingly realistic.

In terms of stories featuring female main characters having and enjoying sex without shame—both female-male and female-female sex—some worth mentioning include Jenny Downham's *Before I Die*, *The DUFF* by Kody Keplinger, *The Fault in Our Stars* by John Green, and *Far from You* by Tess Sharpe.

AMBER: From your perspective as a teen librarian, what's missing?

KELLY: We're missing a lot of sexual identities and sexual preferences in teen-focused media—asexuality, pansexuality, gender fluidity. We need more depictions of sexual exploration and experimentation, especially where the girl's satisfaction and curiosity are at the forefront. I'd also like to see more books about virginity as a choice.

More books featuring characters of all colors and backgrounds are a must. We could also be better about portraying disabled characters and their sexuality in a way that's not just about the mechanics. Recently, writer Kayla Whaley talked about this in a really brave blog post called "Disability, Self-Esteem, and Sex" (disabilityinkidlit.wordpress.com/2013/07/02/kayla-whaley-disability-self-esteem-and-sex).

Teen readers deserve more scenes portraying masturbation, more pleasure, more self-awareness in sex. They deserve more *words* too. It's great to see sexually progressive and empowering sex scenes in the media, but I'd love to see conversations using real and accurate language to talk about abstinence and consent, love and lust, desires and values. This is the kind of language that teens could become comfortable using with sexual partners and peers, and as young adults in a wider world.

Sex is a continual learning process.

There's not one single right way to have a sex life.

Resources

Websites

Scarleteen
A grassroots support organization dedicated to bringing inclusive, comprehensive, and smart sexuality information and help to young people.
www.scarleteen.com

Advocates for Youth
A resource to help young people make informed and responsible decisions about their reproductive and sexual health.
www.advocatesforyouth.org

Sex, Etc.
Honest, accurate information about sex by and for teens.
sexetc.org

Sex+
A frank video series about sexuality with Laci Green.
www.youtube.com/user/lacigreen

Bedsider
An online birth control support network for young women.
bedsider.org

Planned Parenthood
An organization dedicated to delivering reproductive healthcare and sex education to people around the world.
www.plannedparenthood.com

The F Bomb
An online community created by and for young people who care about women's rights.
thefbomb.org

Teen Feminist
The blog of teen activist Jules Spector.
www.teenfeminist.com

Youth Resource
A website by and for lesbian, gay, bisexual, transgender, and questioning young people.
www.youthresource.org

Trans Lifeline
An organization dedicated to the well-being of transgender people.
www.translifeline.org

RAINN: The Rape, Abuse & Incest National Network
An anti-sexual-violence organization that offers support to victims of sexual assault.
www.rainn.org

National Sexual Assault Telephone Hotline
1-800-656-HOPE (4673)

Books

S-E-X: The All-You-Need-To-Know Progressive Sexuality Guide to Get You through High School and College by Heather Corinna (Da Capo Press, 2007)

SEX: A Book for Teens by Nikol Hasler (Zest Books, 2010)

100 Questions You'd Never Ask Your Parents: Straight Answers to Teens' Questions about Sex, Sexuality, and Health by Elisabeth Henderson and Nancy Armstrong, MD (Roaring Brook Press, revised edition, 2013)

Body Drama: Real Girls, Real Bodies, Real Issues, Real Answers by Nancy Amanda Redd (Gotham, 2007)

Dating Smarts: What Every Teen Needs to Know to Date, Relate, or Wait by Amy Lang (Birds + Bees + Kids, 2014)

GLBTQ: The Survival Guide for Gay, Lesbian, Bisexual, Transgender, and Questioning Teens by Kelly Huegel (Free Spirit Publishing, revised second edition, 2011)

Beyond Magenta: Transgender Teens Speak Out by Susan Kuklin (Candlewick, 2015)

Articles

"Teen Sex: It's Complicated," a series of essays by teens about sex, *The Huffington Post*, 2015, www.huffingtonpost.com/news /teen-sex-its-complicated.

"Safe, Sound & Sexy: A Safer Sex How-To," Scarleteen, written 2001, updated 2014, www.scarleteen.com/article/bodies/safe _sound_sexy_a_safer_sex_howto.

"17 Lies We Need to Stop Teaching Girls about Sex" by Julianne Ross, Identities.Mic, 2014, http://mic.com/articles /88029/17-lies-we-need-to-stop-teaching-girls-about-sex.

"17 Lies We Need to Stop Teaching Boys about Sex" by Julianne Ross, Identities.Mic, 2014, http://mic.com/articles /89301/17-lies-we-need-to-stop-teaching-boys-about-sex.

Reassurance for Parents

Many of us are deeply involved in our children's lives. We help with homework. We cheer from the sidelines of soccer fields. We sew costumes for the school play. Day in and day out we are there to help them navigate challenges with friends or difficulties at school.

But when it comes to fostering their understanding and experience of sex—

Gulp!

It can be really hard to know what to do. We don't really want to think about their sex lives, and they don't really want to think about ours. Often it is easier to say nothing at all. But sex isn't a switch that stays in the off position until we have them safely out of the house. No matter how squeamish it makes us, our kids are probably going to eventually have sex.

Girls report sexual thoughts and physical sensations as early as elementary school.[36] The onset of puberty intensifies these feelings as their bodies catch up, ready for the biological imperative to reproduce. By the end of high school, 70 percent of high school seniors are sexually active.[37]

We need to be talking a whole lot more about sex a whole lot earlier, especially because very few schools offer comprehensive sex education (meaning nonjudgmental, complete, accurate, and positive). The curriculum in the twenty-two states that require sex ed is far more influenced by politics than biology.

Typically the focus is on basic anatomy and prevention of pregnancy and sexually transmitted infections, with an emphasis on abstinence. What's missing is a framework for young people to discuss the multifaceted nature of sexuality, the diverse ways we can be sexual with each other, and the development of our sexual selves.

If we as parents are not participating in ongoing conversations about sexuality, the only sources of information available to teenagers are their friends, books, and, increasingly, pornography, a very poor way to learn about sex.

My encouragement to you is this—engage.

Keep an eye out for openings into conversations about sex and sexuality. They are everywhere in our daily lives, from magazine covers in the grocery store to *Modern Family* episodes to news coverage of the latest sex scandal. Each is an opportunity for us to talk about our values and our experiences around sex.

These conversations are not The Talk.

You can forget The Talk. (That's a relief, I know.)

When we take every opportunity to engage our kids in open conversations about healthy sexuality, we are empowering our daughters to ask questions and speak up for themselves in sexually charged situations. They will be able to say *I'm not ready for that* or *You have to use a condom.*

Talking doesn't mean doing. Contrary to what some believe, learning about sex does not make teenagers run out and hook up with the first available partner. Rather, research shows that good sex education delays the onset of sexual activity.[38]

And you are not in this alone. There are some great resources out there. I urge you to check out *For Goodness Sex: Changing the Way We Talk to Teens about Sexuality, Values, and Health* by Al Vernacchio. This book should be on every parent's bedside table. Below is a list of other books, articles, and websites that will help get you started.

I know these conversations might be hard at first but I promise it will get easier. You can do it! And trust me, it's worth it—for us, for our daughters, and for the strong women they are becoming.

Resources for Parents

Advocates for Youth: Parents' Sex Ed Center
A site dedicated to helping parents be positive sex education
resources for teens.
www.advocatesforyouth.org/parents-sex-ed-center-home

Birds + Bees + Kids
Newsletter and resources for parents from sex educator Amy Lang.
www.birdsandbeesandkids.com

*For Goodness Sex: Changing the Way We Talk to Teens about Sexuality,
Values, and Health* by Al Vernacchio (HarperCollins, 2014)

"17 Lies We Need to Stop Teaching Girls about Sex" by
Julianne Ross (mic.com/articles/88029/17-lies-we-need-to-stop
-teaching-girls-about-sex)

"17 Lies We Need to Stop Teaching Boys about Sex" by
Julianne Ross (mic.com/articles/89301/17-lies-we-need-to-stop
-teaching-boys-about-sex)

"Teen Sex Isn't the Problem (But Thinking It Is Sure Is)"
An article in *Everyday Feminism* by Ellen Friedrichs (January 5, 2015).
http://everydayfeminism.com/2015/01/teen-sex

"Teen Sex: It's Complicated"
A series of essays by teens about sex.
www.huffingtonpost.com/news/teen-sex-its-complicated

*Ten Talks Parents Must Have with Their Children about Sex and
Character* by Dr. Pepper Schwartz and Dominic Cappello
(Hyperion, 2000)

Notes

1. "American Teens' Sexual and Reproductive Health," Guttmacher Institute Fact Sheet (May 2014): 1-4.
2. Al Vernacchio, sex educator, interviewed by Amber J. Keyser, September 2014, records in author's personal archives.
3. Amy Lang, sex educator, interviewed by Amber J. Keyser, August 2014, records in author's personal archives.
4. Jo Langford, sex educator, interviewed by Amber J. Keyser, July 2014, records in author's personal archives.
5. Al Vernacchio, *For Goodness Sex: Changing the Way We Talk to Teens About Sexuality, Values, and Health* (New York: HarperCollins, 2014), ix.
6. Vernacchio, *For Goodness Sex*, 55-7.
7. Imogen Parker, "Young People, Sex, and Relationships: The New Norms," Institute for Public Policy Research (August 2014): 21, http://www.ippr.org /assets/media/publications/pdf/young-people-sex-relationships_Aug2014.pdf.
8. Vernacchio, August 2014.
9. Lang, August 2014.
10. Pepper Schwartz, sex educator, interviewed by Amber J. Keyser, July 2014, records in author's personal archives.
11. Langford, July 2014.
12. Langford, July 2014.
13. Langford, July 2014.
14. Schwartz, July 2014.
15. Lang, August 2014.
16. Sarah Mirk, "The Dramatic History of American Sex Ed Films," Bitch Media, June 2014, http://bitchmagazine.org/post/the-suprising-history -of-american-sex-ed-films.

17. Langford, July 2014.

18. "Who Are the Victims?" RAINN (Rape Abuse and Incest National Network), accessed September 18, 2014, https://www.rainn.org/get -information/statistics/sexual-assault-victims.

19. "Who Are the Victims?" RAINN, accessed September 18, 2014.

20. "Rape and Sexual Assault: A Renewed Call to Action," The White House Council on Women and Girls, (January 2014): 1, http://www.whitehouse .gov/sites/default/files/docs/sexual_assault_report_1-21-14.pdf.

21. The White House Council, January 2014, 1.

22. "Statistics," RAINN (Rape Abuse and Incest National Network), accessed September 18, 2014, https://www.rainn.org/statistics.

23. "Statistics," RAINN, accessed September 18, 2014.

24. Vernacchio, August 2014.

25. Lang, August 2014.

26. Schwartz, July 2014.

27. Langford, July 2014.

28. Lang, August 2014.

29. Vernacchio, August 2014.

30. Vernacchio, August 2014.

31. Lang, August 2014.

32. Parker, "Young People, Sex, and Relationships," 22.

33. "American Teens' Sexual and Reproductive Health," Guttmacher Institute (May 2014): 1, http://www.guttmacher.org/pubs/FB-ATSRH.pdf.

34. Langford, July 2014.

35. Lang, August 2014.

36. Sharon Lamb, *The Secret Lives of Girls: What Good Girls Really Do—Sex Play, Aggression, and Their Guilt* (New York: The Free Press, 2001), 2.

37. The White House Council, January 2014, 1.

38. "Comprehensive Sex Education: Research and Results," Advocates for Youth (September 2009): 1, http://www.advocatesforyouth.org/storage /advfy/documents/fscse.pdf.

Acknowledgments

There were three inspirations for this book.

The first was an article written by author Ferrett Steinmetz for The Good Men Project called *Dear Daughter: I Hope You Have Awesome Sex*, a brilliant response to the cultural cliché of dads with shotguns guarding their daughters' chastity. I hope this book succeeds in expanding on his central themes of sex positivity and sexual autonomy.

The second inspiration was a snippet of conversation between two parents that I overheard at my son's soccer game. One mom asked, "Is your son interested in girls yet?" The other responded, "I don't know. I don't want to know." This is typical of many moms I have met in the course of writing this book. Not bad parents, just ill-equipped to help their kids navigate this part of becoming an adult.

The third and most important inspiration was my children. Every word was written with them in mind. I was guided by the hope that they will grow into adults for whom sex is a joyful, positive part of life. They patiently, and with good humor, tolerated "Mom's sex book" and even joined in the conversation.

I am also grateful to Michelle McCann, who championed *The V-Word* from the very beginning; my writing group, the Viva Scrivas; my interviewees, who were so generous with their time and expertise; and to all the parents who found out I was working on this book and grabbed onto it like a lifeline. A huge thank you also goes out to the team at Beyond Words Publishing and Simon & Schuster for the hard work of so many on behalf of this book.

There is always an inner circle. They come bearing wine and Kleenex and encouragement and the belief that I am capable of translating an idea into a real book. Thank you, Kiersi Burkhart, for being the first one on the roller coaster. Thank you, Elizabeth Rusch, for reminding me at every turn that this work was important and beautiful. Thank you, Fiona Kenshole, for making me tea and eggs and being the best knight-in-shining-armor a writer could ask for.

And thank you, Seth Isenberg, for ALL THE THINGS!

The beating heart of *The V-Word* is, of course, the brave women who shared their stories within its pages. Each of them dug deep and then went deeper into experiences that were sometimes painful, sometimes embarrassing, but always honest to the core. I am in awe.

Contributors

About the Author

Amber J. Keyser did not anticipate writing a book about sex for young adults. In fact, she's always been closemouthed about her own sexual history. But through her work on *The V-Word*, she came to believe that engaging in honest conversations about sex with young people is her responsibility as a parent and as a woman. Everyone deserves a deeply pleasurable and wholly chosen sex life. That doesn't happen by accident. Amber's other work includes numerous nonfiction titles and the young adult novel *The Way Back from Broken* (Carolrhoda Lab, 2015). Learn more about her work at www.amberjkeyser.com and on Twitter at @amberjkeyser.

About the Contributors

Molly Bloom is the nom de plume for an author of books for children and young adults. She grew up in a small town in the Midwest but she currently makes her home in New York City. She sports the words of Molly Bloom, from James Joyce's *Ulysses*, on her arm: "and yes I said yes I will Yes."

Kiersi Burkhart was raised as a cowgirl in Colorado, and even though she now lives in Portland, Oregon, she has never forgotten her frontier roots. Her debut middle-grade novel *Shy Girl and Shy Guy* releases in 2016 and taps into her love of stories about bravery, friendship, and horses. Find out more about Kiersi on Twitter at @kiersi and at www.kiersi.com.

"The First Rule of College" Copyright © 2015 by Kiersi Burkhart

Chelsey Clammer has been published in *The Rumpus*, *Essay Daily*, and *The Water~Stone Review* among many others. She is the managing editor and nonfiction editor for *The Doctor T. J. Eckleburg Review*, the essays editor for *The Nervous Breakdown*, and senior creative editor of www.insideoutediting.com. Her first collection of essays, *BodyHome*, was released from Hopewell Publishing in Spring 2015. Her second collection of essays, *There Is Nothing Else to See Here*, was published by the Lit Pub in Summer 2015. You can read more of her writing at www.chelseyclammer.com.

"Ear Muffs for Muff Diving" Copyright © 2015 by Chelsey Clammer

Christa Desir writes contemporary fiction for young adults. Her novels include *Fault Line*, *Bleed Like Me*, and *Other Broken Things*. She lives with her husband, three small children, and an overly enthusiastic dog outside of Chicago. She has volunteered as a rape victim activist for more than ten years, including providing direct service as an advocate in hospital ERs. She also works as an editor at Samhain Publishing. Visit her at christadesir.com.

"I Would Have a Heart" Copyright © 2015 by Christa Desir

Kate Gray is a poet and novelist. For more than twenty years, Kate has tended her students' stories as a teacher at an Oregon community college. Her first novel, *Carry the Sky*, attempts to stare at bullying without blinking. She has published essays and three poetry collections. She and her long-time partner just married and live in a purple house in Portland, Oregon, with their sidekicks, Rafi and Wasco, two very patient dogs.

Justina Ireland enjoys dark chocolate and dark humor, and is not too proud to admit that she's still afraid of the dark. She lives with her husband, kid, and dog in Pennsylvania. She is the author of *Vengeance Bound* and *Promise of Shadows*. Visit her at justinaireland.com.

Laurel Isaac is the pen name of a queer essayist and student in the Pacific Northwest. More of her sexual memoir writing can be found in the collections *Shameless Behavior: Brazen Stories of Overcoming Shame* and *The Big Book of Submission: 69 Kinky Tales.* Laurel's work also addresses issues of queer community, navigating contradictory identities, and how to make queer theory more accessible. Formerly a volunteer and contributor for the feminist sex ed website Scarleteen, she is particularly interested in the intersection of sex education, sex-positive activism, and LGBTQ history. She enjoys hiking and practicing the clown-free circus arts.

Karen Jensen, MLS, has been a young adult services librarian for twenty-one years. She is the creator and administrator for the Teen Librarian Toolbox, where she reviews YA literature and hosts the #SVYALit Project, where young adult literature is used to discuss sexual violence and consent in the lives of teens. In 2014 she was named as a *Library Journal* Mover & Shaker. She is the coeditor of *The Whole Library Handbook: Teen Services* published by ALA Editions in 2014. When she isn't doing librarian things, she is trying to raise two daughters.

Kelly Jensen is a former teen and youth services librarian turned associate editor and community manager for Book Riot (bookriot.com) and she blogs about young adult fiction, reading, and serving teens (stackedbooks.org). She is also the author of *It Happens: A Guide to Contemporary Realistic Fiction for the YA Reader* from VOYA Press. Her writing has been featured in The *Horn Book Magazine, School Library Journal*, and *VOYA*, as well as on *The Rumpus, Rookie*, and *The Huffington Post*.

"It's All in the Choosing" Copyright © 2015 by Kelly Jensen

Sidney Joaquin-Vetromile is the pseudonym for a Filipina American writer and college English instructor. She's been published in The *New York Times, Gawker*, and *The Rumpus*, among other places, and is at work on a memoir and a young adult novel. She divides her time between the Philippines and the United States. Sidney no longer identifies as Catholic but she definitely believes in love.

"Sharing My Anatomy" Copyright © 2015 by Sidney Joaquin-Vetromile

Alex Meeks holds an associate's degree in Young Adult Education from Washington State Community College in Marietta, Ohio, (*cum laude*) and a BA in English from Wells College in Aurora, New York. She lives in Philadelphia, Pennsylvania, where she writes, plays housewife, and surrounds herself with the finest freaks and outcasts the Delaware Valley has to offer.

"Iterum Vivere, to Live Anew" Copyright © 2015 by Alex Meeks

Carrie Mesrobian is the author of three young adult novels: *Sex & Violence, Perfectly Good White Boy*, and *Cut Both Ways*. She teaches teenagers about writing at the Loft Literary Center in Minneapolis. Visit her at www.carriemesrobian.com.

"What Counts" Copyright © 2015 by Carrie Mesrobian

Sarah Mirk is a Portland-based journalist who mostly writes about gender, sex, and social justice. She's the online editor of feminism and pop culture for *Bitch Media* and the host of the podcast *Popaganda*. She is also the author of the open-minded guidebook to dating, *Sex from Scratch: Making Your Own Relationship Rules*.

Sara Ryan is the author of the graphic novel *Bad Houses* with art by Carla Speed McNeil, published by Dark Horse Comics; the young adult novels *Rules for Hearts* and *Empress of the World*, both published by Viking; and various comics and short stories on themes including but not limited to teen angst, female celebrity, joining the military, the 1962 escape from Alcatraz, and circuses. She grew up in Michigan, and now lives in Portland, Oregon, where she works as a librarian and writes at night and on the weekends. She still has all the journals she kept as a teenager. Find her at sararyan.com and @ryansara on Twitter.

Erica Lorraine Scheidt's young adult novel, *Uses for Boys* was a 2014 PEN Center Literary Award finalist, a 2014 Quick Pick for Reluctant Readers, and a Best First Book for Youth by the American Library Association's *Booklist*. A teaching artist and advocate for literary arts programming for youth, Erica is the founder of the Berkeley Writers' Workshop, a creative writing workshop for teens; a founding team member at Chapter 510, a made-in-Oakland creative writing and literacy project; and a longtime volunteer at 826 Valencia, a creative writing center in San Francisco. She was a 2012 Artist in Residence at Headlands Center for the Arts and a 2014 recipient of the Creative Work Fund award. Erica lives with her wife and stepdaughter in Berkeley and spends her days with tenth grade students at Oakland's MetWest High School.

Jamia Wilson is a feminist media activist, organizer, and storyteller. By day, Jamia is the executive director of *Women, Action, and the Media*, and by night, she is a staff writer for *Rookie*, an online magazine. Jamia has been recognized as one of Refinery29's "17 Faces of the Future of Feminism" and as a #SmartFeministofTwitter by the *Ms. Magazine* blog. Jamia's words and works have been featured in *CBS News, Essence, CNN, Forbes.com, Al-Jazeera, Slate, Salon, New York Magazine, The New York Times, The Guardian UK, The Today Show, The Washington Post*, several anthologies, and more. Follow her on twitter at @jamiaw.

"My Name Is Jamia" Copyright © 2015 by Jamia Wilson

About the Sex Educators

Amy Lang helps parents discover talking to kids about "it" doesn't have to be scary or overwhelming. Her engaging, humorous, and inspiring style shows parents how to turn conversations they dread into something they look forward to and wholeheartedly embrace. Through her business Birds + Bees + Kids® Amy helps parents of all beliefs have easy, open and effective conversations about sex with their kids. She is the author of *Birds + Bees + YOUR Kids: A Guide to Sharing Your Beliefs about Sexuality, Love, and Relationships* and *Dating Smarts: What Every Teen Needs to Know to Date, Relate, or Wait*. Amy has been featured in *The Wall Street Journal, The Huffington Post*, and *Babble.com*. Learn more about her work at www.birdsandbeesandkids.com.

Jo Langford is a dad and a Master's-level therapist and sex educator for tweens, teens, and parents in Seattle. For the last twenty years he has worked with teens, parents, and professionals to promote healthy, positive, and safe sexual behavior. He uses information, education, and humor to help families increase their knowledge and self-confidence as a proactive defense against the unfortunate consequences that sometimes accompany teen sexual activity. His mission is to provide healthy social and sexual information to teens and their parents in a multi-pronged approach, consisting of live speaking events, his book *The SEX-EDcyclopedia*, and a series of social and dating-themed apps for the iPhone. Learn more about Jo and his work with youth, parents, and professionals to promote healthy, positive, and safe sexual and social behavior at www.beheroes.net.

Pepper Schwartz received her PhD from Yale University and is professor of Sociology at the University of Washington in Seattle. She is the past-president of the Society for the Scientific Study of Sexuality and the Pacific Sociological Society. She has been honored for her work by the American Sociological Association and been named a Distinguished Alumni from Washington University in St. Louis. She has written twenty-two books and over fifty academic articles. Several of her books have received national recognition, including *The Normal Bar: The Surprising Secrets of Happy Couples* (a *New York Times* bestseller), *Ten Talks Parents Must Have with Kids about Sex and Character* (an Outstanding Book by Mothers' Voices) and *Dating after 50 for Dummies*. She is currently the Love, Sex, and Relationship Ambassador for AARP and serves on the board of Trojan and the Sexual Studies PhD program for the Institute of Integral Studies in San Francisco. Known for her translation of academic work into popular formats, she has appeared often on *Oprah*, *The Today Show*, *CBS Morning News*, *NPR* and other national programs. She also serves as one of the four relationship experts on *Married at First Sight*, a television series on A & E network on the FYI channel. She lives in Snoqualmie, Washington, on a horse ranch.

Al Vernacchio, MS Ed, is the sexuality educator at Friends' Central School in Wynnewood, Pennsylvania. He teaches classes, organizes sexuality programming, provides parent education on human sexuality, and is the faculty advisor for the Gay-Straight Alliance Network. A human sexuality educator and consultant for over twenty years, Al has lectured, published articles, and offered workshops throughout the country on sexuality topics. His work has been featured in "Teaching Good Sex," a November 2011 cover story in *The New York Times Magazine*. In addition, Al is a TED Talk speaker and is the author of *For Goodness Sex: Changing the Way We Talk to Teens about Sexuality, Values, and Health*.